MW00667334

Football Skills & Drills

Tom Bass

Human Kinetics

Library of Congress Cataloging-in-Publication Data

Bass, Tom.
  Football skills & drills / Tom Bass.
       p. cm.
  Includes index.
  ISBN 0-7360-5456-1 (softcover)
  1. Football--Training. 2. Football--Coaching. I. Title: Football
skills and drills. II. Title.
  GV953.5B364 2004
  796.332'07'7--dc22
                                   2004005239

ISBN: 0-7360-5456-1

Developmental Editor: Cynthia McEntire
Assistant Editors: Scott Hawkins, Mandy Maiden
Copyeditor: Alisha Jeddeloh
Proofreader: Pam Johnson
Indexer: Susan Danzi Hernandez
Graphic Designer: Robert Reuther
Graphic Artist: Tara Welsch
Photo Managers: Dan Wendt, Kelly Huff
Cover Designer: Keith Blomberg
Photographer (cover): Getty Images
Photographer (interior): Kelly Huff, unless otherwise noted
Art Manager: Kareema McLendon
Illustrator: Tim Offenstein
Printer: Versa Press

We thank Torrey Pines High School in Carmel Valley, California, for assistance in providing the location for the photo shoot for this book.

Human Kinetics books are available at special discounts for bulk purchase. Special editions or book excerpts can also be created to specification. For details, contact the Special Sales Manager at Human Kinetics.

Printed in the United States of America   10 9 8 7 6 5 4 3

Human Kinetics
Web site: www.HumanKinetics.com

United States: Human Kinetics
P.O. Box 5076
Champaign, IL 61825-5076
800-747-4457
e-mail: humank@hkusa.com

Canada: Human Kinetics
475 Devonshire Road, Unit 100
Windsor, ON N8Y 2L5
800-465-7301 (in Canada only)
e-mail: orders@hkcanada.com

Europe: Human Kinetics
107 Bradford Road
Stanningley
Leeds LS28 6AT, United Kingdom
+44 (0)113 255 5665
e-mail: hk@hkeurope.com

Australia: Human Kinetics
57A Price Avenue
Lower Mitcham, South Australia 5062
08 8277 1555
e-mail: liaw@hkaustralia.com

New Zealand: Human Kinetics
Division of Sports Distributors NZ Ltd.
P.O. Box 300 226 Albany
North Shore City, Auckland
0064 9 448 1207
e-mail: info@humankinetics.co.nz

This book is dedicated to Michele, my wife and partner, who constantly provides positive encouragement and insight for all my writings. I cannot thank her enough.

Contents

Acknowledgments

A word of praise and admiration goes out to the thousands of junior high and high school football coaches who every year give their time, energy, and knowledge to help to shape teenage football players into young adults. I hope this book provides them with information that can enhance their present programs.

Thanks to Cynthia McEntire, my editor at Human Kinetics, who really kept the book moving along, organized the manuscript, and provided special insight into the presentation of the material for teaching football skills. Thanks also to Kelly Huff, our photographer from Human Kinetics, who introduced me to new and wonderful technology that made the selection of the photos for the book an easy, quick, and relaxed experience.

A special thanks to my daughter, Shana, who was always there when Dad needed to discuss the usage and spelling of a word or the wording of a phrase or concept. Her suggestions and ideas were greatly appreciated.

Thanks also to Ed Burke, the head football coach of the championship Torrey Pines High School football team, and the players who gave of their time to help make the book a success. Go Falcons!

Finally, thanks to my good friend and fellow football coach, Harry Johnston, for providing a sounding board for the endless discussion of all things football and life.

Introduction

Young athletes learning to play football within the rules, to the best of their ability, and with great sportsmanship face a tremendous challenge. Football is a demanding game both physically and mentally. It is a game in which desire, determination, and willingness to work hard and to play as a member of a team are very important. Most of all, it is a fun sport.

Although football is the ultimate team sport, on each play every player is involved in an individual battle. Winning or losing this battle determines the success or failure of each play. The challenge is to win as many of these individual battles as possible. Even so, no single player is ever bigger than the team. No individual player can succeed without the aid and contributions of his teammates.

Teamwork starts with the attitude teammates have toward each other. Having fun by kidding around is one of the ways players deal with the pressures of the game, but caring for teammates and giving them encouragement is much more important than spending time joking around.

Teamwork also means treating everyone on the squad with respect, a sign of true sportsmanship. A starting player who knows he will play in every game may find it easier to put in the hours at practice. Each week, this player sees the reward of his hard work and will feel that practice is worth the time and effort. But what about the player who practices just as hard but rarely gets in the game? When I played, these teammates were the ones I came to admire the most. They were the players who ran the opponent's plays and defenses during practice. Their role was to make it possible for the team to succeed. They practiced, got banged up and bruised, but never complained even though they knew they probably would never get a chance to play in the game. Their contribution and reward was to see the starters improve and their team have a chance to win. This group of players represents teamwork at its best.

It is important for coaches to take the time to encourage the players who rarely get to play in the game. These are the players who make it possible for the team to be prepared.

A word of encouragement and appreciation from the coach can mean a lot to someone who rarely gets to play. It is very important to let them know how much their teamwork helps the team to win.

Learning to come together with other players and to work as a team toward a common goal is one of the most important lessons players will take away from the game.

PRACTICING TO IMPROVE

The battles on the field are decided by how players play the game. Understanding and performing the necessary skills and techniques is essential to winning each battle on the field. Mastering these small techniques will greatly increase the level of performance.

In addition, the more a coach and player learn about what their opponent is trying to do, the easier it becomes to defeat his actions. Watching video from a previous game or even seeing an opponent play live, if possible, can help players and coaches gain this knowledge. The more a team sees an opponent and can chart and diagram their offensive and defensive scheme, the better the team can anticipate what the opponent will do and plan successfully to stop them.

Every day in practice coaches will be challenged to help players improve. Coaches should emphasize that the players must do their part by listening carefully and then trying to correctly do what they are asked. Players must concentrate and work hard if they want to get better and for the team to be successful.

During practice, players should watch the more experienced players, listen when the coach corrects what the more experienced players are doing, and remember how it should be done. When they get their chance, less experienced players can recall the instruction given to other players and try to do the skill the correct way. Every minute of practice time needs to be used for learning, even when the player is not involved in the drill.

All players must work on staying strong and in good condition throughout the year. Each player should be physically prepared to play as hard in the fourth quarter as in the first. Players can give themselves this edge by making certain they do extra work when it is needed.

DRILLING FOR SUCCESS

The techniques in this book are explained and illustrated so that the player can work on his own as well as with a coach. Players in every position should practice getting into their stances and working on their starts away from the field.

Some techniques require another person to observe and assist in their practice. This other person can be a teammate who plays the same position. In this way, players can help each other raise the level of their performances and become better players.

When first learning a technique, players should work on their footwork against air. Once they perfect the movement, they can execute the technique at half speed versus a bag and then with a player from the same position. Finally, they can practice the technique against an opponent from the opposite side of the ball at full speed. Early in the season, when conditioning is one of the major goals, players should practice without pads. This is an excellent time to teach and practice footwork drills that do not involve contact as well as to learn assignments.

Competition and contact are two major distractions in learning good technique. Coaches should teach each technique without these two elements at first and then slowly introduce them into the drill.

This book includes technique instruction and drills to help any player improve at any position. Detailed illustrations and photo sequences enhance the text and improve understanding and retention. The first chapter covers two fundamental skills needed by every player—tackling and catching the ball. The following chapters discuss each position in detail, with complete skill instruction, technique photos, and diagrams where appropriate. The book concludes with vital information on the unique positions in special teams play.

My goal is to help you become the very best football coach or player. My priority is to provide the best skills and drills that I have learned throughout my 30 years of coaching. Good luck as you work your way toward becoming a success both on and off the field.

Key to Diagrams

QB	Quarterback
HB	Halfback
FB	Fullback
TB	Tailback
CN	Center
RB	Running back
TE	Tight end
WR	Wide receiver
LT/RT	Left, right tackle
LG/RG	Left, right guard
OG	Offensive guard
OT	Offensive tackle
OL	Offensive lineman
NT	Nose Tackle
K	Kicker
P	Punter
LDE/RDE	Left, right defensive end
LDT/RDT	Left, right defensive tackle
DE	Defensive end
DB	Defensive back
LB	Linebacker
SLB	Strong-side linebacker
WLB	Weak-side linebacker
MLB	Middle linebacker
SS	Strong safety
FS	Free safety
CO	Corner
BC	Ball carrier
TK	Tackler
C	Coach

Skills for All Players

Before moving on to the techniques for specific positions on the field, every player needs two fundamental skills—tackling and catching the ball. Any player might need these skills on the field at any time. The punter may have to make a touchdown-saving tackle of the return man for the other team. A defensive linebacker might have the chance to catch the ball for a drive-stopping interception. A wide receiver may have to make a transition to defense if the other team recovers a fumble or makes an interception. The list goes on and on, which is why this chapter covers the two skills that apply to any player on the field. The chapters on individual skills go into detail on the specific positions, but the following information is a great place for any player to start.

TACKLING

Tackling is to defense what blocking is to offense—it is a vital technique for every defensive player. At the same time, many games are won because an offensive player, punter, or placekicker makes a tackle and stops the opposing team from scoring. Just as vital to good tackling on defense is good, sure tackling by all coverage people on special teams. Special teams are made up of offensive and defensive players, both groups coming together to function as one unit. All players must therefore be able to tackle.

Often the placekicker or punter is the last man in position to stop a long return from going all the way. Therefore kickers need to spend time learning how to get in front of the ball carrier, make contact, and slow the runner down until help can come. It also may come down to just knocking the ball carrier out of bounds at the sideline. The punter and placekicker have to be ready to make the tackle or shove the ball carrier out of bounds if the opportunity arises.

Offensive players who are not part of the special teams will need to tackle after an interception or fumble recovery. On a turnover, the offensive player must quickly go from blocking to tackling. Offensive linemen, who seldom have to make a tackle, may find that they are in perfect position when a defensive player with the ball tries to cut back across the field. They will be able to make the tackle if they are prepared.

In the case of an interception, the first two players to know that an interception has occurred are the intended receiver and the quarterback. Both players are the first to react to the interception, and they can minimize interception return if they have tackling ability. The receiver is in position to quickly chase down the defensive ball carrier because he is usually the closest to the defensive man. The quarterback is the first to see the interception, allowing him to move to where he can intercept the defensive ball carrier and make the tackle or knock the ball carrier out of bounds.

Defensive players are prepared to tackle on every play. All players on special teams must anticipate having to tackle, and offensive players must know that at any moment they may have to switch to defense and tackle. No one on the team can think that he has the luxury of going through the game without having to tackle. Every player on the team must know how to tackle in a safe and sure manner.

Tackling Desire

Good, hard tackling is the heart of any great football team. At times players will make a sure open-field tackle. On these tackles, technique is key. At other times, a player might reach out with one hand and try to grab the ball carrier's jersey while warding off a blocker. Although many tackles happen this way, players must know and understand how to make a good tackle.

The first trait a good tackler needs is desire. The player has to want to get there. On every offensive play, defensive players must go 100 percent to get a piece of the man with the ball. Every coverage player on special teams has to have that great desire to sprint downfield and get in on the tackle. On every interception, three or four offensive players need to go all out to tackle the defensive ball carrier. Every week defensive players and special-teams players will shed blockers and run all over the field to track down a speedy ball carrier. These players never give up until the ball carrier is down or out of bounds. Desire drives these men to run quickly and make the play.

A player puts himself in position to make a tackle by anticipating the movements of the ball carrier and aggressively putting himself between the ball carrier and the goal line. He must recognize and defeat potential blockers before reaching the ball carrier. Defensive and special-teams players are aware of potential blockers, but offensive players must also be taught to look out for blockers so that they can protect themselves as they move toward the ball carrier. Once the tackler has defeated and shed any blocker, he must focus all attention on the ball carrier and adjust his body position to make the tackle using the proper technique.

Tackling Technique

When first learning to tackle, players should start at half speed or less. Only after they have mastered the proper techniques should the speed of any tackling drill increase. Every player is somewhat afraid the first time he lines up to tackle someone. As he learns the techniques and gains more confidence, this fear will become less and less.

Good tackling technique is designed for a picture-perfect tackle. Obviously this rarely happens during a game. The player's major objective when making a tackle is to stop the ball carrier, and it doesn't really matter how he gets it done. He can stop the ball carrier by getting to the ball carrier, grabbing him in any way possible, and keeping him from moving forward until teammates can arrive to help or sending him out of bounds.

The keys to good tackling are getting in the correct position (figure 1.1a) and generating an explosion at the point of impact. The number-one tackling technique is bending the knees. Many beginning tacklers make the mistake of bending at the waist instead of bending at the knees. Bending at the waist causes the back to bow, brings the head and eyes down, and increases the chance of injury.

After bending the knees, the tackler lowers his body in preparation for impact. He keeps his back straight and his head up at all times, focusing his eyes directly on the ball carrier's chest. Every player needs to keep his head up and eyes open during the tackle. The tackler should never lower his helmet, because doing so could result in neck injuries. Players should be reminded repeatedly to make contact with their shoulder pads, never with any part of their helmets.

At the point of impact, the tackler takes off on the foot nearest the ball carrier. If the ball carrier cuts to his left (the tackler's right), the tackler should take off of his left foot (figure 1.1b). When the tackler uses this foot as his explosion foot, his body will be in the correct position: head in front of the ball carrier, eyes focused on the center of the ball carrier's chest. Exploding off the proper foot and taking short choppy steps (leg drive) help the tackler make clean contact with the ball carrier.

a

b

c

Figure 1.1 Tackling technique: *(a)* set up in proper body position; *(b)* drive off the foot nearest the ball carrier; *(c)* make contact with the arms.

When the tackler feels his pads hit the ball carrier's body, he drives his shoulder pads up and through the side of the ball carrier and slams both arms into him (figure 1.1c). The tackler's elbows make the first contact. His front arm makes contact with the ball carrier's belly and his back arm makes contact with the ball carrier's lower back. The tackler automatically raises his hands to the front and back of the ball carrier's jersey and grabs the jersey securely in both hands. The tackler continues his leg drive up and through the ball carrier and finishes by bringing the ball carrier to the ground.

One of the most difficult situations for a tackler is when the ball carrier is running up the sideline and he is the last player in position to make the stop. The difficulty is not the actual tackle but the tremendous amount of open field that the tackler must protect. When in this situation, it is important for the tackler to understand that making the tackle should be the only thing on his mind. If it becomes necessary, he may have to allow the ball carrier 1 or 2 yards up the field in order to ensure that he does not miss the ball carrier completely.

When preparing to make a sideline tackle, the tackler needs to keep the ball carrier between himself and the sideline, approaching the ball carrier at a 45-degree angle. The tackler balances his stance by bringing his feet even and keeping his knees bent as he continues to run in place. He keeps his back straight, his head up, and his eyes focused on the ball carrier. He must stay calm, be patient, and prepare for the ball carrier to go up the sideline or back into the center of the field. In either case the tackler takes a quick, open step in the direction the ball carrier is going. The tackler picks a spot 2 or 3 yards in front of the ball carrier and proceeds to that spot, using it as his tackling point. Once he reaches the spot, he explodes off the foot closest to the ball carrier, driving up and through the ball carrier. If the tackler takes a crossover step instead of an open step, he will not be able to correct his position if the ball carrier cuts back in the other direction.

Players should expect the ball carrier to make head and shoulder fakes to avoid tackles. It is the tackler's job to hold his ground and not lunge at the ball carrier. He should allow the ball carrier to fake in one direction or the other, because the ball carrier must slow down to fake, giving the tackler's teammates time to get there and help make the tackle.

To be a good tackler, remember these key points:

- Good tackling is crucial to a good football team.
- Tackling starts with desire.
- Making the tackle requires proper technique.
- Not every tackle will be perfect.
- The ball carrier is not down until the whistle blows.
- Players must never use any part of the head when making a tackle.

It is a challenge to make an open-field tackle against a good ball carrier. The tackler must anticipate the ball carrier's moves and be ready if the ball carrier tries to cut or run over him. The challenge is worth it, though. There's a real thrill when the tackler sets and drives the ball carrier back with a solid tackle. A good, solid tackle is one of the fun parts of playing football.

Tackling Drills

Defensive players should perform one tackling drill each day they are in pads; kickers and offensive players should tackle at least once a week. It is not necessary or advised to drive the ball carrier to the ground during tackling practice. Players should save that part of tackling for the game.

Angle Tackling

Purpose: To provide all players the opportunity to improve tackling skill and confidence.

Procedure:

1. Line up ball carriers and tacklers 15 yards apart, facing one another (figure 1.2). Position defensive linemen versus defensive linemen, linebackers versus linebackers, defensive backs versus defensive backs, and so on. The placekicker and punter should work with smaller defensive backs.

2. On the coach's command of "Hut," the first ball carrier and tackler advance toward each other at half speed for 5 yards. Only one ball carrier and tackler go at a time.

3. At 5 yards, the ball carrier cuts to his right or left at a 45-degree angle and the tackler mirrors his move. The coach signals the ball carrier which way to cut. The ball carrier should have the ball in the arm on the side of his cut.

4. When the tackler makes contact, the ball carrier gives with the tackle. After the tackle, the tackler goes to the end of the ball carrier line and the ball carrier moves to the end of the tackling line, and the next pair takes their turn.

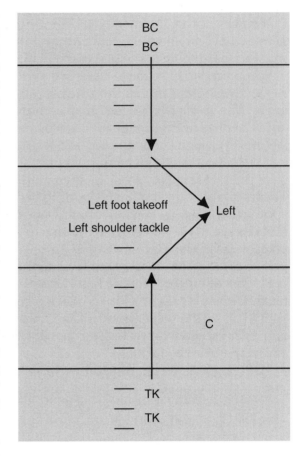

Figure 1.2 Setup for angle tackling drill.

Variations: Once players are tackling properly, all pairs can go at once instead of one pair at a time. After players have run through the drill a number of times, the ball carrier can decide which way to cut.

Coaching Points: As the tackler approaches the ball carrier, he needs to shorten his stride, widen his base, flex his knees, lower his center of gravity, and be ready to explode into the ball carrier. In this position, the tackler can react to any cut the ball carrier might make. When tackling, players should think of driving up and through, not just into, the ball carrier.

Straight Ahead Tackling

Purpose: To provide all players the opportunity to improve tackling skill and confidence.

Procedure:

1. Start with two groups of players 10 yards apart (figure 1.3).
2. When the coach says "Hut," players move toward each other at half speed.
3. The tackler assumes the proper position to make the tackle. The coach tells the tackler which shoulder to use when making the tackle. The tackler steps directly into the ball carrier using the foot on the same side as the shoulder the coach has told him to use. His head slips to the side of the ball carrier.
4. The ball carrier jumps in the air as contact is about to be made.

Coaching Points: The tackler uses the same techniques as in the angle tackling drill except both arms and hands encircle the ball carrier and make contact with the back of his jersey.

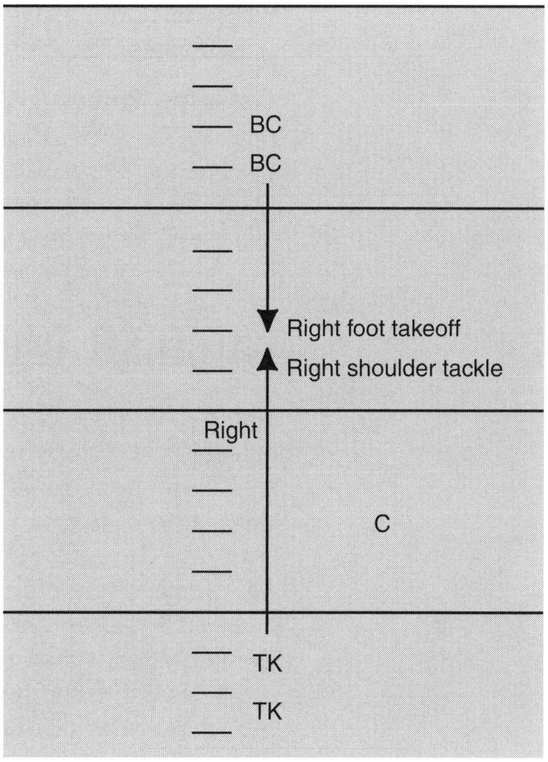

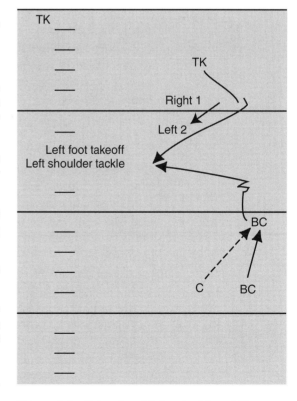

Figure 1.3 Setup for straight ahead tackling drill.

Sideline Tackling

Purpose: To give all players practice making sideline tackles. This is a good drill for punters and kickoff men.

Procedure:

1. The ball carrier and the tackler begin 7 yards apart. The tackler is even with the coach 7 yards from the sideline. The ball carrier is 4 yards from the boundary (figure 1.4). Both players face the coach.
2. The coach begins the drill by tossing the ball to the ball carrier. When he catches the ball, the ball carrier turns and faces up the field.
3. As the ball is in the air, the tackler moves two steps forward and angles his body to the sideline, keeping his feet evenly spaced.
4. The ball carrier moves upfield and cuts to the inside or goes straight ahead without faking.
5. The tackler moves on the ball carrier and tries to tackle him. If he cannot tackle the ball carrier, he should at least try to push the ball carrier out of bounds.
6. After the tackler successfully stops the ball carrier, the two players switch roles and perform the drill again.

Figure 1.4 Setup for sideline tackling drill.

Variation: Once players are comfortable with the drill, the ball carrier can make one or two fakes.

Coaching Points: The tackler should react correctly to the ball carrier's motion, whether he moves to the inside, up the field, or begins to cross. When practicing sideline tackles, it is important to practice on both sides of the field. The coach should have the players work this drill on both sidelines until he feels confident they can make this very important tackle in a game.

CATCHING THE BALL

Like tackling, catching the ball is a basic skill every player on the team needs to learn. In catching, the focus naturally shifts to wide receivers, tight ends, and running backs, who make the majority of catches in a game. However, other players on both sides of the ball may have the opportunity to make a catch, often helping the team win the game. Defensive players may have a chance to make an interception. An offensive lineman may catch a batted ball or a pass when lined up as a tight end in a short yardage or goal-line situation. There is nothing more exciting or fun for the entire team than seeing an offensive or defensive lineman make a catch, secure the ball, and then try to move like a running back.

Some teams design plays in which the running back takes the ball from the quarterback, starts a wide run in one direction, and throws the ball back to the quarterback, who has gone the opposite way after handing off the ball. Sometimes a team fakes a field goal and the holder rolls out one way and then throws the ball back across the field to the placekicker, who has faked a block and gone down the sideline. Often the kicker will be wide open and his ability to catch the ball can lead to a touchdown. It is to a team's advantage if every player knows the right way to catch the ball.

Players must learn to focus all of their attention on the flight of the ball as it moves toward them and block out any distractions from opposing players. To make a reception, players must concentrate on seeing the ball all the way into their hands. Many good receivers talk about actually seeing the point of the ball as it comes through the air and being able to block out the other players around them. Every pass is theirs and they demonstrate tremendous desire and pride in catching every ball thrown in their direction.

Catching a pass is one skill that players can improve with technique instruction. In the heat of a game, players will not have the time to think through each step when making a catch. Therefore it is important for players to spend time on and off the practice field working on receiving. To understand the mechanics of a reception, players must first understand the elements of the catch that they need to practice.

One of the most important skills is the positioning of a player's hands (figure 1.5). The way he sets his hands for a catch changes based on the flight and location of the ball. When players drop passes, it is usually because they positioned their hands wrong or they did not extend their arms far enough to see both the ball and their hands at the same time. When the receiver focuses on the flight of the ball but keeps his hands near his body where he cannot see them, he has to coordinate his hand position with the flight of the ball in an instant, at the moment of the catch.

Correct hand position allows the receiver to see both the ball and his hands, giving him more time to adjust before the ball arrives.

To catch a ball at the level of the numbers on his jersey or lower, the receiver uses the palms-up technique (figure 1.6). He places the little fingers of his hands together, turning the palms up. He opens both hands and spreads his fingers and thumbs to form a secure, oval catching area for the ball.

The same palms-up catching technique is used to make an over-the-head or over-the-shoulder reception. When a receiver is running up the field and must make a reception over his head or shoulder, he should reach high and back with his hands so he can see his hands and the ball together (figure 1.7).

When the receiver must catch a ball that is coming directly at him and is shoulder-height or higher, he should use the thumbs-together hand

Figure 1.5 When the receiver's hands are in the correct position, he can see both the ball and his hands.

position (figure 1.8). For this type of pass, the receiver puts his thumbs together with his palms facing out and slightly down. The fingers of both hands are open and spread, forming a cradle for the catch. The receiver catches this pass while facing the ball, not looking over his shoulder.

Figure 1.6 Palms-up catching technique.

Figure 1.7 Hands in position for an over-the-head reception.

Figure 1.8 Thumbs-together hand position.

Figure 1.9 Wrists cocked back.

To keep from dropping the ball, the receiver cocks both wrists (figure 1.9). Even when their thumbs and fingers are in the correct position, many receivers have trouble making a reception when the ball is shoulder-high or above because their palms are turned down to the ground. Rather then catching the ball when it reaches their hands, they merely deflect the ball to the ground. To correct this error, it is important for a player to cock his hands back so that his palms are turned up, not down.

When making a reception to either the right or left, regardless of how high the ball is, it helps a receiver to position his hands so that the palm of the hand on the side of the ball acts like a baseball mitt and comes in contact with the point of the ball, stopping its flight (figure 1.10).

During a game, a single receiver may have few opportunities to catch the ball. He must be prepared so when the opportunity does come, he is able to make the catch. When the ball comes his way, the receiver must have his hands in the proper position, focus completely on the ball, and see the ball and his hands as he makes the catch. Immediately after making the catch, the receiver must secure the ball. Once the ball reaches a receiver's hands, he immediately brings the ball into his body with both hands. The hand on the side of the reception covers the front tip of the ball as he pulls it snug against his ribs. The uncovered tip of the ball is secure in his armpit.

The receiver also needs to be aware of defenders and expect to be hit. All players, but especially receivers, must be taught that any time they touch a ball, whether they catch it or drop it, they probably will get hit. They need to concentrate on the flight of the ball, make the reception, and instantly secure the ball close against their side.

Catching is a skill everyone needs to know. Wide receivers, tight ends, and running backs must be prepared to make a reception on any pass play called in the huddle. Defensive players must be ready to make an interception any time the quarterback goes back to

Figure 1.10 Using one hand as a mitt to stop the ball.

throw. All other players should learn to catch the ball in case the opportunity ever comes up in a game and they are in position to make the catch.

Palms-Up Catching

Purpose: To reinforce proper catching technique when the ball is at the numbers or lower.

Procedure:

1. Players line up on a yard line 5 yards away from the coach and face the coach.
2. The coach throws the ball to the first player in line.
3. The player makes the catch by placing the little fingers of both hands together, turning the palms up, opening both hands, and spreading the fingers and thumbs of both hands to form an oval catching area for the ball.
4. The coach throws the ball to the next player in line.

Coaching Points: Make certain that the receiver extends his hands away from the body and that his little fingers are touching. His palms should be up and not angled straight down toward the ground. He should be able to see his hands and the ball at the moment of the catch.

Thumbs-Together Catching

Purpose: To reinforce thumbs-together catching technique when the ball is shoulder-high or higher.

Procedure:

1. Players line up on a yard line 5 yards away from the coach and face the coach.
2. The coach throws the ball to the first player in line.
3. The player makes the catch by putting his thumbs together with his palms turned out and slightly back, opening both hands and spreading his fingers to form a cradle for the catch.
4. The coach throws the ball to the next player in line.

Coaching Points: Make certain that the receiver extends his hands away from the body and that his thumbs are touching. His palms should be open to the ball and cocked slightly back away from the ground. He should be able to see his hands and the ball at the moment of the catch.

Practice Receiving

Purpose: To reinforce proper catching technique.

Procedure:

1. When a player is learning hand position it helps to start without the ball. The coach faces the receiver and calls out the side (left or right) and the location of the catch: knee, thigh, waist, chest, shoulder, or above the head.

2. The receiver stands in a comfortable position and then reaches out with his arms, simulating a pass arriving at different locations.

3. Once players achieve the correct position, add a ball to the drill.

Variation: After working on passes of various heights to both the left and right of the receiver, the receiver works on catching simulated passes at various heights directly in front.

Coaching Points: The player's hands must be placed correctly for each reception and his arms must be extended so that his hands are in view.

2

Quarterback

The quarterback leads the offense. This position carries a great deal of responsibility and can be loaded with pressure. In addition to being a good leader, the quarterback must be an effective and quick decision maker and have the athletic ability to handle the physical demands of the position. Finally, the quarterback must be able to keep the team on course when it is playing well and rally the team when the going gets tough.

QUARTERBACK MINDSET

The quarterback needs to know his offense and the defenses he will face. A team's success depends on how he studies the game and prepares mentally for each contest.

The quarterback should keep a written record of the plays that the team will use that week and the down and distance when they will most likely be called. During the week, he should study the list—the game plan—away from the field. He must be confident that he knows how to call each play and what his responsibilities are on each play.

Once a quarterback is more experienced it is vital that he not only have an understanding of his own position, but that he also knows the responsibilities of the other 10 players on the offense. He may not understand the techniques each player uses, but he should be aware of their assignments on each play. This requires study by the quarterback away from the field.

The thing that makes the difference among average, good, and great quarterbacks is not physical ability but mental toughness. Great quarterbacks stay focused on winning the game, never give up, and never quit. This is the mental toughness that coaches and teammates want and need from their quarterback. Quarterbacks need to spend time on the mental aspect of the game in addition to physical skills.

It is the quarterback's responsibility to understand the entire running and passing game. He must know when a receiver will come open and where and when to deliver the ball. The quarterback also needs to be able to read the defense and react appropriately. Reading defenses is a skill that takes years to perfect. The coach can begin by teaching the quarterback to recognize whether the defense is playing a man-to-man or a zone-pass defense. The quarterback can then learn to identify who will be the primary and possibly the secondary receiver for each style of coverage.

It is never too early for the coach to teach the quarterback that he is the leader of the offense and that the other players on the offense look to him for direction. He must understand that it is his responsibility to understand the offense; know his assignments as well as those of the other 10 offensive players; take charge of the huddle, calling each play with authority and confidence; be positive and offer encouragement to every player on the team; listen to his coaches; and think about the team first and his performance second.

The quarterback position is so complex that it is challenging for veterans, much less novices. To simplify things, it helps to shorten the list to three primary challenges: calling plays, knowing the formations, and throwing to the correct receiver. Individuals may experience more problems in one area than the others. It is essential for the quarterback and coach to stay positive and continually work to improve the areas the quarterback has trouble grasping.

The quarterbacks coach must be adept at tutoring players who are best suited to be quarterbacks. The coach must teach the quarterback how to conduct himself in the huddle and in other aspects of the role not directly tied to executing plays. When the quarterback steps into the huddle, he should take over and convey a sense of confidence to the other 10 players. It is his job to speak forcefully, making certain that he calls the play correctly, that the players understand the formation, and that every player hears the play, formation, and snap count. He then breaks the huddle and briskly gets the players up to the line and in the proper formation.

BASIC QUARTERBACK SKILLS

The quarterback must be able to both run and pass the ball. Although some skills, such as footwork, vary depending on the play, certain skills are basic to the position regardless of whether a pass play or running play has been called. The quarterback needs to master these techniques—using the proper stance, controlling the snap, and securing the ball—to play the position proficiently.

To perform these skills, a quarterback must be in good physical condition. When the fourth quarter comes, the quarterback needs to step into that huddle ready to go. If he looks beat and out of shape, his teammates will feel the same way and their play will reflect it.

Stance

The quarterback has to move in a number of directions. He has to go forward, right, and left; retreat from the line to pass; and angle away from his starting position. His beginning stance must allow him to move easily in all of these directions, and it must help him perform the physical movements required to play the position. A quarterback has to be able to assume a proper stance without even thinking about it.

To assume the proper stance (figure 2.1), the quarterback stands up straight with his feet even and shoulder-width apart, toes pointed straight ahead. He keeps his weight balanced on both feet, his back straight, and his head up. The quarterback needs good vision downfield so he can see the defense, and his stance must provide him with a clear view of the field.

The quarterback begins to squat by bending his knees. He moves his shoulders forward until his head and shoulders are slightly in front of his hips. He extends his arms out in front and brings his hands together directly in front of and just below his crotch. He places the heel of his passing hand on top of the heel of his nonpassing hand and extends and separates his fingers and thumbs. He spreads his hands apart so that they are wide enough to receive the ball from the center.

All quarterbacks must practice getting into the stance until it becomes comfortable. When the quarterback practices without a center, he may not bend his knees enough or place his hands as low as he will need to when the center is there. The quarterback should always try to get his hands at the proper height and the correct bend in his knees, even when practicing without a center. He will discover that the correct stance does not fatigue him as much when he is actually taking the ball from the center.

a   b

Figure 2.1   Quarterback stance: *(a)* side view; *(b)* front view.

Snap

It is vital for every quarterback to realize the importance of the snap. Every successful offensive play begins with the quarterback receiving and controlling the ball from the center.

Once the quarterback is in a comfortable stance that allows him to move the way he needs to, he works with the center to guarantee a proper exchange of the ball. The quarterback must realize that the center cannot change his height. It is the quarterback's responsibility to adjust the bend in his knees to ensure that his hands fit snugly in place (figure 2.2a). The quarterback's top hand should always be placed in the exact same location. He can guarantee this by placing his middle finger directly against the center seam of the center's shorts or pants. Once the top hand is in place, the heels of both palms should be touching, his hands should be open, and his fingers should be open and spread apart. The quarterback presses up slightly to let the center know that he is ready for the snap. The quarterback must be ready to secure the ball with his bottom hand the instant the center snaps it to him (figure 2.2b).

When practicing the snap, both the center and the quarterback need to practice moving one or two steps in the direction the play calls for. This makes practice more gamelike, helping the quarterback develop a feel for how the ball will be snapped during a game. On a running play, the center may step straight ahead, to his right,

a

b

Figure 2.2 Snap to the QB: *(a)* QB set up behind CN; *(b)* QB secures the ball with his bottom hand.

or to his left depending on the play called. The quarterback may move in the same direction as the center or in a different direction.

The quarterback needs to spend extra time with the center working on the snap for passing plays. When the center drops back in pass protection, he moves with the quarterback, not away. The center may lower his butt in order to move backward. This is an entirely different action than in running plays, and the quarterback needs to be prepared for it. Not only must the quarterback secure the ball, but he has to move quickly away from the line of scrimmage to give the center enough room to make his block.

Even without the center, the quarterback can work on the snap. Another quarterback can get down on a knee in front of the quarterback and bring the ball up sideways from the ground into the quarterback's hands. Even though this is not the same as having a center, it is good practice for a quarterback who is working on gripping the ball and moving right or left or dropping back.

Many young quarterbacks are fine with the snap until they get into an actual game. At that moment, two things often occur:

1. The center is anxious to block and snaps the ball slightly harder and not exactly in the proper position.
2. Anxious about the contact that happens in actual game conditions, the quarterback pulls out faster than he has practiced and is unable to secure the ball properly.

The quarterback can overcome these problems by practicing taking the ball over and over again, anticipating and knowing where his center is going. For any offensive play to have a chance for success, he must be able to get the ball securely from the center.

Ball Security

Once the ball comes up from the center, the quarterback grips the ball with both hands and immediately brings it in to his belly. He keeps the ball secure near his body until it is time for the handoff or he is ready to pass. His passing hand is over the laces and his other hand is on the opposite side of the ball. He exerts the most pressure on the ball with the middle finger of his passing hand. From this position, he can either hand the ball off or set up to pass. If the ball does not come up correctly during the snap, he needs to make an adjustment to get the laces in the proper position if he is going to pass. He should keep the ball in both hands for as long as possible.

Stance

Purpose: To reinforce proper quarterback stance so that it becomes automatic.

Procedure:

1. Quarterbacks line up facing the coach.
2. When the coach points to a player, the quarterback steps forward and assumes his stance.
3. The coach checks the player's stance to make sure he is using the correct technique: feet are even and shoulder-width apart; weight is balanced on both feet; back is straight; head and shoulders are slightly in front of hips; arms are extended; fingers are spread.
4. Once the quarterback is in his stance, the coach directs him to take a step up, right, left and back. The coach gives the players the snap count and then one by one has each quarterback move into stance and stay in that position as he goes through the entire cadence call.
5. Once all quarterbacks are taking a proper stance, they can set up as a group to shorten practice time.

Coaching Points: Observe each quarterback from the front and the side to make certain that his body is in proper alignment. Check each quarterback for balance and observe if he is leaning too far forward or is leaning back with the weight on his heels.

Snap With Movement

Purpose: To solidify the connection between the center and quarterback during the snap.

Procedure:

1. The center and quarterback assume their positions.
2. The coach calls a play and the blocking for the center. You can call plays by using your terminology or using a descriptive manner (dive right or left with drive blocking, sweep right or left with reach blocking to the side of the play, a drop-back pass with pass blocking). However, it is best to call the play using your team's terminology to reinforce what the players will hear in the game. The idea is to have the center move with but opposite the quarterback's movement, driving straight ahead and dropping back to pass protect.

3. The quarterback gives the cadence, and the center snaps the ball to the quarterback.

4. Both the quarterback and center take the initial steps of the play.

Coaching Points: When practicing the snap with the center, both the center and the quarterback need to practice moving one or two steps in the proper direction for the play called. This helps the quarterback get the feel of how the ball will come to him during a game.

Adjusting to the Ball

Purpose: To give the quarterback experience adjusting to the ball from the snap.

Procedure:

1. The drill starts with the center snapping the ball to the quarterback or a player or coach handing the ball to the quarterback from the ground. The person snapping the ball should change the position of the laces so that the quarterback is forced to make the adjustment on the move.

2. The quarterback takes the snap and, holding the ball in both hands, adjusts it so that the laces are in the right location for him to grip the ball to pass (figure 2.3).

3. The quarterback starts his drop.

Figure 2.3   Quarterback adjusting to the ball.

Coaching Points: This drill takes only a few minutes each day, but it pays incredible dividends in a game. In the game, the center gives the quarterback the ball with the laces ready to be gripped. However, game circumstances may cause the center to alter the ball's positioning. The quarterback must be ready to adjust to the ball on the snap to prevent fumbles.

RUN PLAYS

Every quarterback needs to be able to successfully execute both running and passing plays, even if his offense focuses more frequently on one or the other. For running plays, the quarterback needs to work on footwork, handoff technique, and faking.

It is the quarterback's responsibility on all running plays to make certain that he delivers the ball to the ball carrier. He must know the path the running back is going to take and the exact spot where the exchange should take place. Until the handoff occurs, the quarterback must protect the ball by securing it in both hands and keeping it against his body.

When the quarterback is handing the ball to a running back, he approaches the handoff point with the ball in both hands. As he nears the running back, he extends the ball, taking away the hand closest to the ball carrier. The quarterback is now in position to place the ball securely to the ball carrier's midsection.

Each play requires different footwork in order for the quarterback and the running back to reach the handoff point at the proper time. The quarterback has to adjust to the size of each running back, the same way he has to adjust to the size of each center on the team. Every dedicated pro quarterback practices his footwork on running plays. The challenge for the young quarterback is learning the different footwork patterns for various running plays. A quarterback who neglects this skill usually is half a step short. He often overextends his arm and fumbles the handoff.

Based on the type of offense the team uses, the quarterback has four or five different paths he can take to reach the handoff point. The footwork for each running play is different, so it is important for the quarterback to work on each path equally. On all plays, he must receive the ball from the center, secure it firmly in both hands, and bring it into his body at belt level.

The handoff is the quarterback's responsibility and should become automatic. It is important that the quarterback turn his head as quickly as possible and focus on the exact spot where the handoff will take place. He must get the ball to the running back at the proper point on the field in a secure manner on all running plays.

For a running play in which the running back comes straight down the line (figure 2.4), the quarterback first takes a very short directional cheat step with the foot on the same side as the handoff. He turns his hips in the direction of the cheat step and points them down the line, allowing his upper body and head to turn with his hips. The quarterback takes a longer second step with the other foot along the line of scrimmage. He must be in position to extend his arms, his hand, and the ball to the handoff point as the second foot makes contact with the ground. To complete the handoff, he removes the hand nearest the ball carrier's body and places the ball firmly to the ball carrier's belly.

For a running play in which the quarterback needs to get the ball to a deep back who approaches the line at an angle (figure 2.5), the quarterback's footwork again starts with a short step back with the foot on the same side as the handoff. The actual handoff takes place deep in the backfield, so this first step must be back. His second, longer step with the opposite foot carries him at an angle away from his original position. From here the rest of the handoff is the same.

A play in which the quarterback hands off to a running back who is coming across the formation on an off tackle or sweep play requires a change in the quarterback's footwork. For his cheat step, he steps back with the foot opposite from the running back's direction. He takes his second, longer step back from the line, opening his body to put him in position to make the handoff to the back. When the quarterback executes this type of handoff, his body should be turned toward his goal line and away from the line of scrimmage (figure 2.6).

Figure 2.4 Quarterback hands off to running back coming straight down the line.

Figure 2.5 Handoff to deep back approaching at an angle.

Figure 2.6 Handoff to running back coming across the formation.

The footwork is the same when the quarterback executes a reverse pivot for a handoff or pitches the ball to the running back (figure 2.7). He takes a short step up with the foot on the side of the play. He pivots around on this foot with his second step. When he is in the pivot, he loses sight of the line of scrimmage for an instant. The action of the handoff is the same as on other running plays.

When the quarterback pitches the ball (figure 2.8), he needs to adjust the location of the ball in his hands. As he pivots, the quarterback brings the ball to the hip on the same side as the play. On his second step, he quickly extends both arms and uses an underhand toss to send the ball to the running back.

For a smooth exchange, the quarterback should always put the ball to the center of the runner's belly. Most fumbles in the exchange occur when the ball only reaches the near hip of the runner or when it is too low and makes contact with the running back's thigh. Following a handoff, the quarterback must continue for at least three or four steps, setting up just as he would if it were a play-action pass.

Figure 2.7 Reverse pivot.

Faking the handoff is an important tool for the quarterback. Good fakes keep the defense off guard and make it easier to execute key plays at crucial moments in the game. One of the most important skills for the quarterback is attention to detail when giving or faking the ball to the ball carrier.

There are two main techniques for faking the handoff: the one-hand fake and the two-hand fake.

Figure 2.8 Pitching the ball to the running back.

For the one-hand fake (figure 2.9), the quarterback needs to do the following:

1. Move the ball to the hand nearest the running back.
2. Secure the ball to the quarterback's hip on that side.
3. Quickly put his empty hand to the ball carrier's belly.
4. Remove his hand and continue his steps into his drop.

If the quarterback and the ball carrier practice this motion enough, the running back may be able to deceive the defense into thinking he is running with the ball after the fake handoff.

For the two-hand fake (figure 2.10), the quarterback keeps the ball firmly in both hands. As he reaches the handoff point, he uses both hands to extend the ball to the ball carrier and then quickly pulls it back. Because the defensive players actually see the ball going to the ball carrier's midsection, this is often the most effective way to fake.

Figure 2.9 One-hand fake.

Figure 2.10 Two-hand fake.

When the quarterback fakes with both hands, he also has greater control of the ball, lessening the chance for a fumble. The running back must not grip down on the ball.

Quarterbacks survive and become great because of the running game. To be successful, every quarterback must learn, understand, and practice the footwork, handoff techniques, and fake handoff techniques that are necessary for him to become more effective. On running plays the quarterback's job after handing off to the running back is to carry out his fake. An option-offense quarterback's contribution to the running game is much greater.

It is beneficial to videotape the quarterback's work on each handoff. This allows the coach and the quarterback to review the quarterback's footwork and body action on each handoff and make any necessary corrections.

Coming Down the Line

Purpose: To reinforce proper footwork during a running play from split position.

Procedure:

1. The quarterback and halfback line up in split position. It's best to have a center snap the ball to the quarterback, but if a center isn't available the next quarterback in line can lift the ball to the quarterback executing the drill.
2. The quarterback calls the snap and executes the handoff to the halfback.
3. The halfback carries out the play, running at least 10 yards downfield with the ball. The quarterback carries out the fake and sets up to pass.

Coaching Points: In this type of drill, it is important for the quarterback to call out the cadence and for the players to start at the same time. Check to see that the players come together at the proper point and that the ball is placed firmly to the ball carrier's belly. Watch the quarterback and make certain that he sets up properly after executing the handoff.

Angle Footwork

Purpose: To reinforce proper footwork during a running play from I position.

Procedure:

1. The quarterback and tailback line up in I position. It's best to have a center snap the ball to the quarterback, but if a center isn't available the next quarterback in line can lift the ball to the quarterback executing the drill.
2. The quarterback calls the snap and executes the handoff.
3. The tailback carries out the play, running at least 10 yards downfield with the ball. The quarterback carries out the fake and sets up to pass.

Coaching Points: Check to see that the quarterback's first step is away from the line, allowing him to move into the backfield. Because the tailback is coming from an I position 7 yards from the line, the quarterback and the tailback may not come together smoothly at first. Always check to see that the tailback's path is correct and that he is not getting to the handoff spot too soon.

Making the Handoff on a Sweep

Purpose: To reinforce proper handoff technique for a sweep play from split position.

Procedure:

1. The quarterback and halfback line up in split position. It's best to have a center snap the ball to the quarterback, but if a center isn't available the next quarterback in line can lift the ball to the quarterback executing the drill.
2. The quarterback calls the snap and executes the handoff for a sweep.
3. The halfback carries out the play, running at least 10 yards downfield with the ball. After the handoff on a sweep, the quarterback fakes a bootleg action to the opposite side rather than dropping back to set up to pass.

Coaching Points: Make sure the quarterback gets his head around and quickly focuses on the halfback. He should place the ball firmly to the ball carrier's belly. After the handoff, the quarterback continues to move to the outside of the formation away from the halfback's path at a depth of 7 yards from the line. During a game, the quarterback should look to see if anyone is watching his fake as he moves to the outside.

Turning on a Reverse Pivot

Purpose: To practice the execution of a handoff during a reverse pivot.

Procedure:

1. The quarterback and fullback line up in far position. The fullback is directly behind the quarterback 4 yards from the line. It's best to have a center snap the ball to the quarterback, but if a center isn't available the next quarterback in line can lift the ball to the quarterback executing the drill.
2. The quarterback calls the snap and executes a reverse pivot to make the handoff to the fullback.
3. The fullback carries out the play, running at least 10 yards downfield with the ball. The quarterback carries out the fake and sets up to pass.

Coaching Points: Make certain the quarterback takes a short step up with the foot closest to his final direction in order to ensure that he secures the ball before making his pivot. The quarterback must turn his back to the line of scrimmage and turn his head and body with his second pivot step. Check that he is locating the fullback as he pivots around and that he keeps the ball secure in both hands at the belt area until he is ready to make the handoff. Once the quarterback makes the handoff he should drop back to set up to pass.

One-Hand Fake

Purpose: To teach and reinforce proper one-hand faking technique.

Procedure:

1. The quarterback and running back line up in a predetermined play. No other players are necessary unless a center is available to start the play by making the snap.

2. The quarterback calls the snap and makes a one-hand fake.

3. The running back carries out the fake for 10 yards. The quarterback drops back to pass.

Coaching Points: The quarterback should move exactly as he would if he were handing the ball to the running back. Any variation of steps or rising up will only alert the defense that he is faking. Check to see that the quarterback puts his empty hand to the running back's belly and that the running back leans forward and closes his arms as if he were receiving the ball.

Two-Hand Fake

Purpose: To teach and reinforce proper two-hand faking technique.

Procedure:

1. The quarterback and running back line up in a predetermined play. No other players are necessary unless a center is available to start the play by making the snap.

2. The quarterback calls the snap and makes a two-hand fake.

3. The running back carries out the fake for 10 yards. The quarterback drops back to pass.

Coaching Points: The quarterback must securely grip the ball with both hands to guarantee that the running back does not jar it loose. The quarterback must quickly place the ball to the belly of the running back and then instantly bring it back to his own belt area. The running back can lean forward, but he must not close his arms around the ball.

PASS PLAYS

The passing game is a vital part of football. The quarterback must know the defense, call the right play, and deliver the ball to the open receiver consistently. A learning quarterback should start with drop-back passing and then move on to play-action passes and passing on the move. Finally, the quarterback needs to spend a few minutes each week throwing the ball on the run while scrambling out of the pocket. All of these passing skills can improve with hard work and practice.

Throwing Technique

All quarterbacks want to pass the ball. A quarterback's success as a passer depends a great deal on the amount of time he devotes to learning the proper mechanics for throwing the ball. One of the most important ways for the quarterback to grow is to master the throwing techniques.

It is better to take the time to go back and review the basics of throwing if the quarterback is having trouble accurately passing the ball. Do not allow a quarterback to continue throwing bad passes. Before passing, the quarterback needs to master securing the ball in both hands, taking the drop the play requires, and executing the footwork needed to prepare to pass. The quarterback also needs to know how to grip the ball and the actual movement that he should go through as he passes the ball.

Figure 2.11 Quarterback grips the football.

Figure 2.12 Quarterback uses his nonpassing hand to secure the ball when dropping back to pass.

Every good pass starts with the grip on the ball. Without a proper grip, the throw lacks the accuracy or velocity the quarterback needs and wants. The size of the quarterback's hands in relation to the ball will cause some variation in the way he is able to grasp the football. Regardless of the size of his passing hand, the quarterback grips the ball near the center (figure 2.11). He places the index or first finger of his throwing hand near the tip of the ball, off the laces and across the seam where the laces are located. He places the middle and third fingers across the laces. The fingertips of these two fingers are on the surface of the ball, not on the laces. The little finger just reaches the laces of the ball. The coach should check the quarterback's grip during every practice.

The quarterback should feel the most pressure between the ball and his passing hand just behind the center point on the back of the ball. Depending on the size of his hand, the quarterback may need to slightly adjust the base grip, but he must keep the pressure in the same location.

Until the quarterback is ready to actually pass the ball, he should keep his nonpassing hand on the ball, placing it lightly on the underside of the football to keep the ball more securely in his grasp (figure 2.12). Most quarterback fumbles occur during the exchange from the center or when the quarterback removes his nonpassing hand and starts running with the ball in only one hand. The quarterback does not have complete control of the center snap exchange, but he must have total control when he is going back to pass. He must keep both hands on the ball whenever possible.

The quarterback's passing motion begins with a step forward on the foot opposite his passing arm (figure 2.13a). The quarterback aims the toes of this lead foot directly where he wants the ball to go. The lead foot is very important—the quarterback must step directly toward where he is going to pass the ball. The quarterback's body is now in position. With this step, the quarterback's entire body begins to point at the spot where he wants to deliver the ball. At this moment, his lead foot and hips are aimed at the target.

At the same time the quarterback steps with his lead foot, he releases his nonpassing hand from the ball and brings his passing hand back, bending the elbow on his passing arm (figure 2.13b). The ball is above his shoulder pads and slightly behind his helmet.

When the quarterback begins to deliver the pass, his hips and shoulders move toward the target, ahead of his passing arm and hand (figure 2.13c). An accurate passer who passes with touch and velocity always begins the passing movement with his entire body, not just his arm. The quarterback needs to understand that arm speed and ball velocity result from using the entire body to make the throw.

As the quarterback's body moves forward toward the passing area, his shoulder, passing arm, and hand also begin to move forward (figure 2.13d). His elbow is bent and the ball is held high. The quarterback allows his passing arm to finally come forward as he delivers the pass.

As the passing arm comes forward, the quarterback's lower arm passes over and in front of his elbow. The hand and the ball extend forward, and the ball comes out of his hand in a nice, tight spiral. When the quarterback releases the ball, he points his hand and fully extended passing arm directly at the passing target. After the release, the passing hand rotates to the inside and the palm of the passing hand finishes the passing motion turned down to face the ground (figure 2.13e).

Figure 2.13 Passing motion: *(a)* QB steps forward with the lead foot; *(b)* he brings his passing hand back; *(c)* his hips and shoulders move toward the target; *(d)* his passing arm comes forward; *(e)* he releases the ball and finishes the passing motion.

Quarterbacks need to practice throwing to make it one smooth motion. At the moment of release, every part of the quarterback's body should point directly at the passing target. His body should be in a direct line to the passing area. Lead foot, hips, shoulders, head, eyes, and passing hand should all point in the same direction.

When beginning to teach the passing motion, the coach may want to have the quarterback practice setting up and going through the entire passing sequence without the ball until it becomes comfortable and the coach feels that he is doing it correctly every time. The quarterback needs to step to throw to all areas of the field, not just to the middle or to the side of his passing hand.

Drop-Back Passing

When the quarterback perfects the running game and play-action pass, the drop-back pass attack will be that much better. For any passing game to be successful, the timing of the quarterback's throws must be as exact as possible. Good timing during a passing play depends on two people, the receiver and the quarterback. The receiver contributes to the timing of the pass by running his routes at full speed and at the proper depth. The quarterback contributes to the timing by having disciplined drops for each pass and delivering the ball to the receiver at the correct time. The quarterback must know the proper drop and work on his footwork so that he has a consistent drop each time he moves away from the line of scrimmage.

Each drop has to become second nature for the quarterback. Every time he sets up to pass, it is important that his steps and the movements of his body remain constant. During the drop, the quarterback must control the ball before releasing the pass, have a smooth, consistent throwing motion, and release the ball the same way on every pass as much as possible.

As the quarterback learns to drop correctly, he should not throw the ball, focusing instead on footwork and timing. Once he starts throwing, that becomes the main focus, and in the beginning the quarterback needs to concentrate solely on his footwork.

A center is not necessary, but it is important that the quarterback start each drop by taking a very short step up with the foot opposite his passing arm. When the center joins in the practice, the quarterback will find that this slight step up guarantees that he gets a good exchange, stays with the center, and gets a good grasp of the ball.

The quarterback should use crossover steps as he drops away from the line (figure 2.14). Each drop has a specific number of steps that the quarterback takes before setting up and stepping to throw the ball.

To deliver the pass using a quick, efficient motion, the quarterback needs to be sure the ball is in the correct position during the drop. Before the quarterback starts the drop, the coach should be sure the quarterback has a correct grip on the ball, has the ball securely in both hands, knows to keep the ball at the middle of his chest during the entire drop, and understands that his arms should move forward and back in a normal motion.

Figure 2.14 Crossover step.

The quarterback needs to know the surface of the field. On a normal, dry playing field, the quarterback's final step can be somewhat longer and can be used to stop his movement away from the line. When playing on a wet or loose field, the quarterback must shorten his final step to keep his feet under him and prevent a slip as he sets to throw the ball.

Three-Step Drop. The quarterback should start by learning the three-step drop. This drop is used for all short pass patterns, which are pass patterns run at 4 or 5 yards from the line of scrimmage, such as quick out, hitch, or slant. With all these passes, timing is essential. The quarterback must take the steps and deliver the ball without hesitation if the pass is to be completed.

The quarterback does not count the first, slight step forward he uses in each drop. After the slight step, he steps away from the line of scrimmage with the foot on the same side as his passing hand. He follows this with a crossover step with the other foot and then a step with the foot on the same side as his passing hand. The quarterback's third step should stop his momentum and allow him to step in the direction he is going to throw the ball.

Five- and Seven-Step Drops. A quarterback needs a five- or seven-step drop for medium and deep pass routes, or pass patterns run at over 5 yards. As a general rule, the deeper the pattern the receiver runs, the deeper the quarterback's drop.

The quarterback's goal on any pass play is to deliver the ball to the receiver on time and at the point in the receiver's pattern at which the receiver has the best opportunity to make the catch. The quarterback needs to have very disciplined drops if his timing is to be correct.

For both the five- and seven-step drop (figure 2.15), the quarterback takes both the first step away from the line of scrimmage and the last step with the foot on the same side as the quarterback's passing hand. He follows his first step with a crossover step. He continues the drop by alternating feet until he has taken the appropriate number of steps.

The quarterback should use a five-step drop on all medium pass routes: in, out, hook, cross, delay, quick post, and deep up. When he takes the final step in the drop, he should be nearly 7 yards from the line of scrimmage.

When a receiver is running an out pattern, the quarterback should expect him to make his break toward the sideline at 12 yards. When the quarterback takes the final step, he immediately starts the throwing motion by stepping with his front foot at a point 9 yards directly in front of the receiver's path. This is the amount of space the receiver normally covers while the ball is in the air.

The up pattern is actually a deep pass pattern but is thrown from a five-step drop. The quarterback must be prepared to throw the ball the minute the receiver moves up the field and gets even with the defensive back, usually at 12 yards. The quarterback should throw the pass 10 yards in front of the receiver and 5 yards to his inside so that the receiver has a chance to run directly under the pass to make the catch.

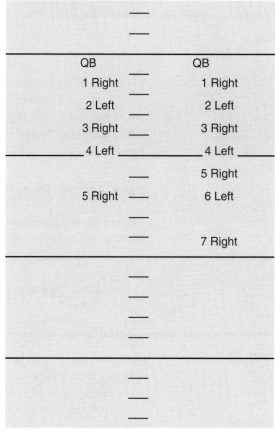

Figure 2.15 The QB is nearly 7 yards from the line of scrimmage after a five-step drop and 9 yards away after a seven-step drop. (Illustration shows steps for a right-handed passer.)

Figure 2.16 Plant step.

The seven-step drop should be used for deep pass routes, such as post, corner, and comeback. The seventh step of the drop should take the quarterback 9 yards away from the line of scrimmage as he sets up.

Throwing a corner route requires the quarterback to take a full seven-step drop. He must be prepared to lead the receiver with the ball toward the corner of the field on the sideline. In a post pattern, after the receiver starts toward the center of the field at 10 yards, he quickly breaks to the outside to the corner of the field. The quarterback must anticipate this path change and be ready to step and throw the ball 12 yards in front of the receiver's path. Ideally he throws the ball in front of and to the outside shoulder of the receiver.

On both of these drops, the quarterback sprints away from the line of scrimmage at a much greater speed than in the three-step drop. Because of this speed, the final step, or the plant step, is crucial (figure 2.16). The quarterback extends the final step, unless he is on a wet or loose field, to stop his momentum away from the line of scrimmage. Then he gets in position to set up for his delivery. When on a wet or loose field, the quarterback shortens the plant step and keeps his feet under him to keep from slipping on the plant step or just as he tries to throw the ball.

Once the quarterback stops his momentum away from the line of scrimmage, he brings his front foot back slightly in order to plant both feet under his hips and get in position to begin the throw. The quarterback is in perfect position to step to any area of the playing field to deliver the pass. He holds the ball securely with both hands at chest-height. He gathers his body and stands tall with both feet under his hips, and then he begins the passing motion.

Play-Action Passing

As the quarterback begins to master the mechanics of drop-back passing, he can start working on the footwork and mechanics of passing the ball after faking a run. Play-action passing requires even more work, but it is an important part of a team's attack.

Everyone has seen a great quarterback move to a running back and appear to hand off the ball. All the fans plus a majority of the defense are certain that it is a running play. Then at the last second the quarterback quickly removes the ball, sets up at 7 yards, and delivers a perfect pass to an open receiver. Play-action passing, or throwing a pass after faking a run, can be a tremendous weapon for any offensive team.

A successful play-action pass is the result of a combination of actions by the quarterback and the ball carrier. Success requires coordination between the quarterback and the running back. When the quarterback is handing off the ball, he must sell the pass to the defense. How well he carries out his fake not only sets up the play-action pass in subsequent plays, but also may cause the defense to hesitate, which helps the running back.

It all starts with selling the fake. Although success ultimately depends on a number of factors, it begins with the quarterback's execution of actual running plays. When he hands the ball to the running back, he must carry out his assigned fake. His body movement should be the same whether the play is a run or a pass. The coordination between the quarterback and the running back should look the same in this first phase of the play-action pass.

The running back's effectiveness in faking the handoff, hitting the hole, and driving on a play-action pass can greatly affect the success of the play. The running back's fake is not enough, though. If the quarterback is going to have the time he needs to complete the pass, his fake of the handoff must be just as convincing as the running back's fake.

Successful play-action passing is based on offensive deception that results in defensive indecision. Everyone on the offensive team must try to convince the defense that the play is a running play, because the goal of the offense is to make the defenders play the run. Convincing the defense that the play is a run slows down the pass rush, keeps the linebackers near the line of scrimmage, and ideally causes at least one defensive back to leave his coverage and come up to tackle the running back, leaving the receivers open.

The quarterback uses the same footwork for play-action passes that he uses for running plays. When faking a toss to the running back from an I formation, the quarterback takes a short step up with the foot on the same side as his final directional fake. The quarterback turns his back to the line of scrimmage and gets his head and body around with his second pivot step. From this position he extends both his hands and fakes tossing the ball to the running back, who goes through the motions of making a catch. Once the quarterback

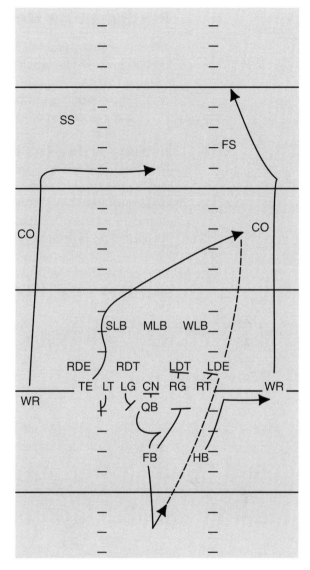

Figure 2.17 Fake FB 34, QB play-action TE cross.

brings the ball back to his belly, he begins his crossover drop for three additional steps, taking him 7 yards from the line of scrimmage. This type of play-action pass should be used with any of the medium patterns run by a receiver.

At the point at which the quarterback would normally put the ball to the running back's belly for the run, he fakes the handoff (figure 2.17). The coach needs to tell the quarterback whether to use a one- or two-hand fake. Once the quarterback completes the fake, he sets up at the proper depth using a three- or five-step drop. He gathers his feet under him to be in position to throw just as he would on a drop-back pass.

Most play-action passes are thrown from inside the pocket, giving the quarterback time to set his feet properly and go through the normal throwing motion. The quarterback should practice making the fake, setting up, and stepping to pass to all areas of the field. He must be sure to maintain the proper mechanics of the throw.

The time a quarterback spends practicing play-action passes can greatly enhance his ability. It should be an important part of the workout program.

Passing on the Move

After learning play-action passing, the quarterback should progress to movement passing, where he will learn to move out of the pocket to one side or the other and deliver the ball while he is on the move.

A majority of the quarterback's passes are either drop-back or play-action passes. Both have predetermined steps and a certain spot at which the quarterback sets up, and both provide the quarterback time to step and throw at his target. When throwing on the move, however, all that changes. The quarterback does not have the benefit of setting up and going through his normal throwing motion, so throwing on the move requires him to think in a different way.

The offense may have different types of passes that require the quarterback to move out of the pocket and throw on the run. These are designed plays, not instances in which he is forced out of the pocket by defensive pressure. For example, in a sprint-out or roll-out pass (figure 2.18), the quarterback follows the movement of one or more of the offensive backs to one side of the formation. Other movement passes include waggle or bootleg plays (see figure 2.19), in which the backs go in

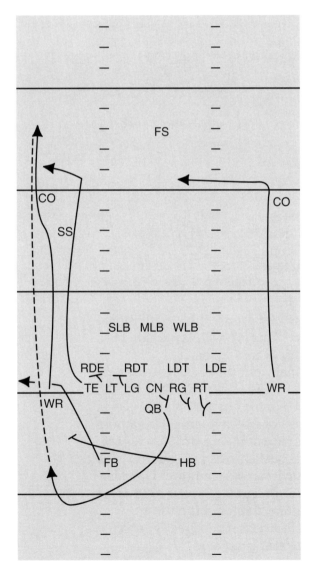

Figure 2.18 QB roll out left.

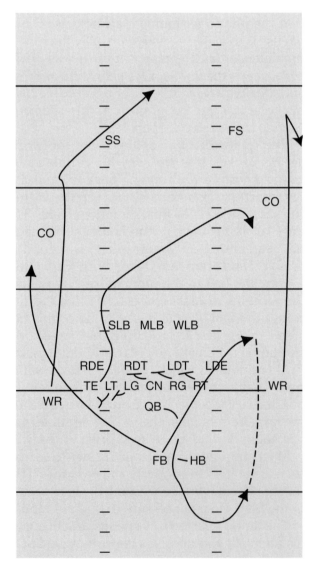

Figure 2.19 Fake HB 29 sweep, QB bootleg right.

one direction and, after faking the run, the quarterback comes out with the ball on the other side of the formation.

If the quarterback knows how to throw while on the run, the type of movement pass will not matter. The first thing the quarterback must do is get his hips turned down the field, pointing directly at the target. He begins to move his body in the direction of the pass by stepping with the foot opposite his throwing arm. He must take this lead step directly toward his target.

When the quarterback is moving to the same side as his passing arm, getting turned is much easier than moving in the other direction to throw the ball. When the quarterback moves to the side opposite his throwing arm, he needs to go a little deeper to give himself room to get turned upfield before delivering the ball.

When the quarterback's hips and opposite foot lead the throw, the passing arm is free to come through in a normal throwing motion. The quarterback needs to carry the ball high. He moves forward during the entire throwing motion and keeps his momentum moving at the target. He delivers the ball as his body continues to move over the lead foot, and he finishes with a continuing step, using the foot on the same side as his passing arm.

Quarterbacks who get into trouble when throwing on the move don't turn their hips and bodies toward the target; instead their hips point at the sideline. They end up trying to throw across their bodies or stopping and trying to deliver the ball to the receiver with only their arms.

Center and Quarterback Pass Play

Purpose: To reinforce to the quarterback the importance of moving back on passing plays so the center has room to block in pass protection.

Procedure:
1. The center and quarterback set up.
2. The center and quarterback execute the snap and then execute their moves for a drop-back pass.
3. The center moves with the quarterback, and the quarterback backs away far enough to allow the center to move into pass protection. The center retreats off the line 2 yards while the quarterback takes his normal five-step drop, reaching 7 yards in depth. During this drill the quarterback should not throw the ball.

Coaching Points: Check the exchange point between the center and the quarterback to make certain that the ball is brought up properly to the quarterback's hands. The quarterback should take a short cheat step up with the foot farthest from his passing hand so that he can securely grasp the ball. The center should not step back too far as he makes the snap. This prevents any chance of stepping on the quarterback's foot.

Three-Step Drop

Purpose: To reinforce the proper technique for the three-step drop.

Procedure:
1. The coach lines up on the defensive side of the ball, facing the quarterback and the center. If no center is available, another quarterback can lift the ball to the quarterback to start the drill when the snap count is called out.

2. The coach tells the quarterback the pattern and the snap count.

3. The quarterback takes his stance, calls out the cadence, takes the snap, and executes the three-step drop.

4. As the quarterback drops back, the coach points in the direction of the pass. The quarterback steps in that direction and goes through the throwing motion without releasing the ball.

Coaching Points: Although there is no receiver in the drill, the coach needs to make certain the quarterback practices stepping to all areas of the field—right, center, and left—after setting up with the three-step drop.

Five- and Seven-Step Drops

Purpose: To reinforce the proper technique for the five- and seven-step drops.

Procedure: This drill is the same as the previous one, except the quarterback determines on his own if he is to take a five- or seven-step drop based on the pass pattern called by the coach. As he drops, the quarterback looks at the coach to get the direction of the pass. The quarterback doesn't need to throw the ball after he goes through the correct drop and throwing motion.

Coaching Points: Although there is no receiver in this drill, it is important for the quarterback to practice stepping to all areas of the field (right, center, and left) after he has taken the five- or seven-step drop and set up properly.

Arm Strength

Purpose: To increase arm strength and reinforce that arm speed and ball velocity result from using the entire body to make the throw.

Procedure:

1. Two quarterbacks stand 10 yards apart (figure 2.20).

2. Each quarterback takes turns stepping and throwing three passes to the other quarterback.

3. After three passes, one quarterback moves back an additional 5 yards, creating a 15-yard separation. The quarterbacks throw three more passes to one another.

4. The quarterbacks continue the drill, increasing the distance by 5 yards after three passes each, until one of the quarterbacks starts to change his natural body motion to make the pass or releases the ball at a too-high trajectory, causing it to float in the air. When one of these actions occurs, the quarterbacks return to the previous distance and throw five passes each at this distance. If at all possible, try to match up quarterbacks who start with similar arm strength.

Coaching Points: The coach should never allow a quarterback to keep practicing a labored throw. Once one of the quarterbacks shows a breakdown in technique, all the quarterbacks should return to the previous distance where they threw with ease. Quarterbacks should keep a daily record of the distance and the number of passes thrown correctly.

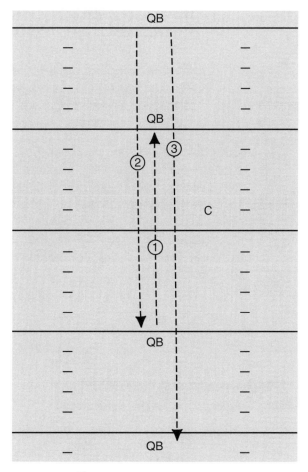

① First set of passes – 10 yards
② Second set of passes – 15 yards
③ Third set of passes – 20 yards

Figure 2.20 Setup for arm-strength drill.

Multiple Quarterbacks, Multiple Receivers

Purpose: To increase the number of passing attempts for each quarterback during practice.

Procedure:

1. This drill requires three quarterbacks and three receivers. Two quarterbacks line up on hash marks, and one quarterback lines up in the center of the field. A tight end gets in position in the center of the field, and two wide receivers line up, one near each sideline (figure 2.21).

2. The coach calls out a pass route to the three receivers. The outside receivers run the same route; the tight end runs a companion route.

3. The quarterback in the center of the field calls the cadence for the snap count. On the snap, all three quarterbacks execute the proper drop for the pattern called. The receivers run the correct route.

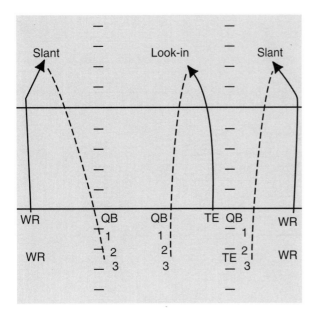

Figure 2.21 Setup for multiple quarterbacks, multiple receivers drill.

4. The quarterbacks on the hash marks pass to the wide receiver on their side. The quarterback in the center of the field passes to the tight end.

5. After throwing the passes, the quarterbacks rotate from left to right so everyone has the opportunity to throw a variety of passes in all directions to a number of receivers.

Coaching Points: Start with short passes that use a three-step drop and progress to medium and deep routes that use a five- or seven-step drop. Quarterbacks should try to throw as many passes as possible during practice time. Keep correction and instruction to a minimum during the drill, especially for the receivers. This drill is primarily designed to increase passing opportunities for the quarterbacks.

Turning and Stepping to the Target

Purpose: To give the quarterback experience passing while on the move.

Procedure:

1. The quarterback lines up behind the center. The coach tells the quarterback the direction he should move after taking the snap. Another quarterback, acting as a receiver, is positioned downfield at 12 yards, near the sideline, and facing the quarterback.

2. After receiving the snap, the quarterback moves to the right or left, taking a path that puts him at least 7 yards off the line of scrimmage.

3. As the quarterback moves to the outside, he brings the ball up to chest level and prepares to make the throw.

4. The quarterback positions his body so that he steps directly at the receiver as he starts the throwing motion and releases the ball. Move the receiver to different positions on the field so that the quarterback must adjust his path to prepare to throw.

Coaching Points: The quarterback should move to the right and left and execute the pass on the move. His front foot, hips, chest, and shoulders should point at and move directly toward the target so that his passing arm can come forward in a normal passing motion.

3

Offensive Lineman

Offensive lineman is one of the least glamorous positions on the offensive team, yet it is one of the most important. The position requires a player who possesses mental toughness in addition to physical skills and is satisfied with little public recognition.

The three qualities that set great offensive linemen apart are enormous personal pride in what they do, a tremendous desire to dominate the players on defense, and self-motivation.

To play the offensive line, a player needs to be able to do the following:

1. Get into a proper stance
2. Get off on the snap
3. Execute the drive, hook, and angle block
4. Work with other players to double team and combination block
5. Block a linebacker
6. Pull to lead the ball carrier
7. Set up for pass protection

The most important skill for any offensive lineman is blocking. One play may require the offensive lineman to drive a defensive player off the line, and the next may require protecting the quarterback as he drops back to pass.

STANCE

An offensive lineman has to block to his right, left, or straight ahead. On some plays, he has to move laterally behind the line of scrimmage. On pass plays, he retreats off the line to protect the quarterback. The beginning stance must be balanced, allowing him to perform all of these movements.

The stance may vary depending on the team's style of offense. Most offensive linemen use a three-point stance. A four-point stance is more appropriate when a team uses blocking that is more straight ahead, or for short-yardage and goal-line blocking. The offensive linemen use a two-point stance when on a team that throws the ball a great deal of the time.

In all three stances, there are some constants. In any stance an offensive lineman keeps his head up and his eyes focused straight ahead. He keeps his shoulders even and his back straight. He never leans to one side or the other. When an offensive lineman leans, he gives the defensive players the advantage of knowing where he is going before the play begins. He does not rock back on the heels.

A three-point stance gives the offensive lineman the ability to move in all directions. To get into a three-point stance (figure 3.1), the offensive lineman begins by standing straight up with his feet even and shoulder-width apart, the toes pointing straight ahead. Keeping his head up and his back straight, he bends at the knees until he can rest his forearms on his inner thighs. Next, he takes a small step back with his outside foot. The toes of the back foot are even with the

Figure 3.1 Three-point stance.

middle of the front foot. His forearms resting on the inner thighs, he reaches out with the hand on the same side as his back foot and places the hand straight down and slightly in front of his shoulder. His shoulders are even, and his weight is evenly distributed on both feet, especially if the direction of his first step changes with each play. He has little or no weight on his down hand.

If he opens his hands with his fingers up instead of putting one hand on the ground, he is in a two-point stance (figure 3.2). The two-point stance is ideal for retreating off the line to protect a pass play.

The four-point stance (figure 3.3) is designed for drive blocking straight ahead or short-yardage plays. To get into a four-point stance, the offensive lineman starts with both forearms on his thighs. Next, he reaches forward with both arms, placing his hands on the ground slightly in front of his shoulders. His shoulders are even, his weight is on his hands, and the heels of both feet are off the ground. He now is in a good position to drive forward.

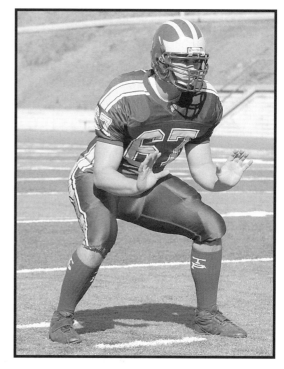

Figure 3.2 Two-point stance.

SNAP TIMING

Because the defensive players are so close, the offensive lineman needs to develop an explosive start off the line of scrimmage. Players must condition themselves to concentrate on the snap count. It is important for offensive linemen to stay square in their stances until the snap.

When exploding off the line, the offensive lineman should take short steps and move forward quickly (figure 3.4). This allows him to position himself into the defensive

Figure 3.3 Four-point stance.

Figure 3.4 Exploding off the line.

man. When blocking the defensive man, the offensive lineman must remember to maintain a wide base, keep his back straight, keep his shoulders low and square, and move with his head up and eyes focused on the target.

One important goal when working on the start is to keep the momentum moving forward in one fluid motion. To develop this smooth, powerful motion, the player must have a wide base and take short, powerful steps. The offensive lineman must prepare for the defensive player to charge forward when the play begins, because contact occurs much more quickly with a defensive man than it does when practicing with a blocking bag or sled. If the offensive lineman takes long steps, there is a good chance he will have a foot in the air when contact occurs, and it will be much harder to get the block.

When a play is called in the huddle, the offensive lineman mentally reviews his assignment as he moves to the line of scrimmage. Once he is at the line and in his stance, he concentrates on the quarterback's voice and prepares to react instantly when the snap count is called. Being late when moving on the snap usually results in a defender winning the battle, while moving early results in a penalty that moves the offense back 5 yards.

Crowd noise, defensive movement, and fatigue are three factors that often keep an offensive lineman from being mentally prepared to move on the snap. Blocking out crowd noise requires complete concentration on the quarterback's voice. Defensive movement may cause the lineman's blocking assignment to change before the snap, requiring the offensive lineman to adjust to a new assignment. Maintaining physical endurance all during the season can help prevent fatigue.

Getting Off on the Snap

Purpose: To develop an explosive start off the snap.

Procedure:

1. This drill requires only the coach and the offensive linemen. The linemen go one at a time.
2. The offensive lineman lines up in his stance (two-, three-, or four-point).
3. When the coach gives the snap count, the lineman charges straight ahead for 5 yards.
4. After each player performs the drill correctly one at a time, they can go through the drill as a group.

Coaching Points: Offensive linemen should use short, quick steps off the line. They should move forward in one smooth motion.

BLOCKING

For an offense to enjoy success, they must have good blocking. A majority of this blocking comes from the offensive linemen. While every player's role is important, no offensive player—quarterback, running back, or receiver—will have a chance to do his job if the offensive line does not block the defense successfully.

Offensive linemen have to block while moving straight ahead (drive block), to their right or left (hook block and angle block), in combination with other linemen (double team block and combination block), while moving laterally behind the line (pull and drive block), and when setting back off the line to protect the quarterback as he drops to throw (pass-protection block).

Drive Block

On a drive block, the offensive lineman blocks the defensive lineman who has set up in front of him. The drive block is a fundamental technique that each offensive lineman must master. The goal of the drive block is to move the defender back off the line of scrimmage. Offensive linemen use drive blocks on most quick hitting plays and on short-yardage and goal-line situations when a defensive player is lined up in front of them.

To begin the drive block, the offensive lineman takes a short step up with his back foot the instant he hears the snap (figure 3.5a). This quick step gets his momentum moving toward the defensive player. He maintains a wide base, keeps his feet spread apart, and takes short, rapid steps during the entire block. If his feet are too close together, it is much easier for the defender to push him aside.

As he moves forward, the offensive lineman keeps his shoulders square and his back straight. To avoid injury and keep the defender in his vision, he keeps his head up and his eyes looking directly at his target.

Most defenders line up directly across the line from the offensive linemen. The defensive lineman comes forward as the ball is snapped, and the offensive lineman should expect to make contact when his second step hits the ground (figure 3.5b). He continues driving with both feet the instant he makes contact, keeping his momentum moving forward.

When the offensive lineman makes contact, he drives forward into the defensive lineman with his arms and hands (figure 3.5c). To get maximum leverage and force, he keeps his elbows close to his ribs. The inside position usually wins. The palms of both hands make contact with the middle of the defensive man's body in a strong, forceful manner.

Although the offensive lineman makes contact with his shoulder pad and hands, his legs do the majority of the work. At the instant his hands make contact with the defender, he pushes his hips forward and upward, gathering his legs under him while keeping his feet driving with short, choppy steps (figure 3.5d). Blockers who are just learning to drive block tend to stop moving their feet at the moment of contact. To keep his feet driving and finish the block, the offensive lineman should pick a spot two or three feet past the defensive man as his goal.

Good offensive linemen take great pride in their ability to drive block. Players can practice the drive block by blocking into a big bag or blocking sled, but they need to realize that when they block a real defensive player, the defensive player will be moving, not standing still.

At the start of the play, a linebacker lines up 3 to 4 yards off the line of scrimmage, directly opposite the offensive lineman. The offensive lineman needs to use a drive block, though contact occurs after the offensive lineman has taken a few steps (figure 3.6). The two major differences between this style of drive block and the drive block previously discussed are that the offensive lineman has to run to get to the defender, and the defender has a greater opportunity to move to his right or left as the offensive lineman comes forward to block him.

To successfully block a linebacker, the offensive lineman must get a quick start. He must know the snap count and take a fast step directly at the backer with his

Figure 3.5 Drive block: *(a)* short step on the snap; *(b)* momentum moves forward as contact occurs; *(c)* offensive lineman plants his hands on the defender's chest; *(d)* offensive lineman keeps moving his feet as he pushes the defender off the line.

back foot. The blocker should keep a wide base and stay low as he moves across the line. The closer he comes to the linebacker, the wider his base should be and the shorter his stride.

As the blocker prepares to make contact, he bends his knees and lowers his hips slightly in preparation for the block. His back is straight, and he keeps his head up and his eyes focused on the center of the linebacker's chest. The blocker initiates the block with the large muscles of the legs, coming up and through the defender in an explosive motion and keeping his legs moving.

Hook Block

On a hook block, the offensive lineman blocks a defensive player who is lined up on his outside shoulder. The primary objective of a hook block is to stop the defender

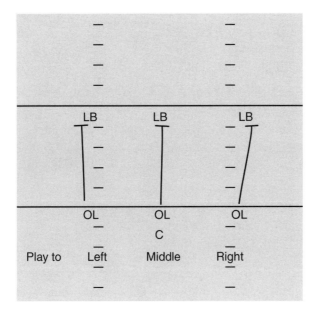

Figure 3.6 Linebacker sets up 3 to 4 yards off the line of scrimmage in front of offensive lineman.

from penetrating the line of scrimmage, because then the offensive lineman can stop the defender's pursuit and drive him back. Offensive linemen use this block most often on wide running plays to their side of the field.

On the snap the offensive lineman takes a very short position step with the foot on the same side as the defensive player. He takes this step laterally down the line of scrimmage. This step puts the offensive lineman's body in front of the defender and moves him into position for the block (figure 3.7a).

For his second step, the offensive lineman steps with his other foot directly at the defender (figure 3.7b). All the power for the block comes from this step. As the second step drives into the ground, the offensive lineman forces his far arm into the defender's chest. As he gets into position in front of the defender, the offensive lineman lifts the arm on the side of the block into the defender's chest (figure 3.7c). Once he gets his body directly in front of the defender, he is able to drive the defensive player off the line of scrimmage. When the offensive lineman has stopped the defender's movement across the line, he continues to drive with his feet, using short, powerful steps as he would in a drive block.

Angle Block

In an angle block, the offensive lineman blocks a defender who is lined up in front of the offensive player to his right or left. When the play begins, the defensive lineman focuses on another offensive player, so his reaction to the angle block is secondary. The offensive lineman must execute the angle block with speed and quickness so that he drives into the defender before the defender can react.

The offensive lineman also needs speed and quickness to stop the defender's penetration across the line of scrimmage. When first learning the angle block, linemen often make the mistake of stepping to the spot where the defensive man lined up, not to where he will be once the play begins and he moves forward. The defender charges straight ahead, and the offensive lineman must anticipate this forward charge when moving to make the block.

Figure 3.7 Hook block: *(a)* offensive lineman in front of defender, ready to block; *(b)* offensive lineman steps at defender; *(c)* offensive lineman drives into defender.

a

b

c

To start the angle block, on the snap the offensive lineman takes a short step down the line of scrimmage with the foot nearest the defensive man he is to block (figure 3.8a). This step puts him in position to get his head in front of the defender. It also turns his hips and allows him to continue the block into the side of the defensive man's body. The offensive lineman does not narrow his base with this step, and he keeps a good bend in both knees.

The second step positions the offensive lineman's head, shoulders, and body squarely into the side of the defensive man (figure 3.8b). The offensive lineman's back remains straight and his head and eyes stay up. He stays low and keeps his eyes on the defender. This second step generates a majority of the power for the block.

As his second step hits the ground, the offensive lineman explodes into the defender with the shoulder pad that is on the same side as the second step. As his shoulder pad makes contact, he drives the palm of the hand on that side into the defender's ribs with as much power as he can (figure 3.8c).

Figure 3.8 Angle block: *(a)* offensive lineman steps laterally toward defender; *(b)* offensive lineman makes contact with defender; *(c)* offensive lineman drives into the defender.

a

b

c

From this initial explosion point, the offensive lineman maintains a wide base and continues to drive his legs in short, powerful steps. At the same time he thrusts his hips forward and down, allowing him to drive up and through the defender. His goal is to drive the defender down the line of scrimmage away from the spot where the ball carrier is going to run.

The offensive lineman should practice this block to both his right and left until he can execute it correctly in both directions. Because of the element of surprise and because the offensive lineman can attack the defender from the side, the angle block is one of the most devastating blocks for an offensive lineman.

Double Team Block

The drive, hook, and angle blocks are performed by a single offensive lineman. In a double team block, two offensive players work together to block one defensive

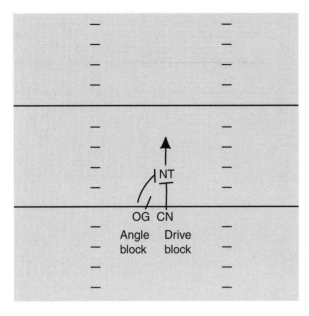

Figure 3.9 Center and guard double team block.

player. The double team (figure 3.9) is the most powerful block an offense can direct at a defensive player. The combined size, weight, and power of two offensive players are directed at one defender. The defender should never win this battle. A good defensive player often reacts to the double team by merely dropping to the ground.

The double team block is a combination of two blocks with slight adjustments. The offensive player directly in front of the defender uses a drive block, and the offensive player who blocks from the side of the defender uses a modified angle block. Combining these two individual blocks results in a double team block.

Depending on the type of offense the team uses, a double team block may involve any offensive lineman and the tight end. In practice, the coach must work with every combination of offensive players who might execute this block together.

On the snap of the ball (figure 3.10a), the drive blocker takes a short position step with the foot on the same side as the angle blocker and explodes into the defender. The angle blocker takes a short position step with the foot on the same side as the drive blocker. After this short position step, the angle blocker explodes into the defender. Once the two blockers take the position steps, they should be next to one another (figure 3.10b). From this position, the two bring their hips and shoulders together. Moving together side by side, they should be able to overpower the defender (figure 3.10c).

The drive blocker has the responsibility to prevent penetration by the defender. The angle blocker provides the added explosion to guarantee movement of the defensive player. The goal is to move the defender laterally down the line of scrimmage, back toward his goal line. When the offensive linemen accomplish this, they not only block the defender but they stop any other defender from pursuing the ball carrier.

Based on the defender's position and the offense used, an offensive player may be either the drive blocker or the angle blocker on the double team. Even the tight end may need to be the drive blocker if a wing back is the angle blocker in short-yardage and goal-line situations. All offensive linemen and tight ends need to practice both parts of the block.

Combination Block

In combination blocking, two offensive linemen block two defensive players. The two players to be blocked are usually a defensive lineman and a defensive linebacker who are lined up next to each other. When executing the combination block, the offensive linemen should come off low on the snap. They need to keep their feet moving and take short, choppy steps. Offensive linemen should never cross their feet, because crossing the feet causes the offensive lineman to lose his base and power.

Offensive linemen use the combination block against stunting or slanting defenses. In a combination block, the offensive tackle and guard can work together or the guard and the center can work together. In either case, the combination block starts

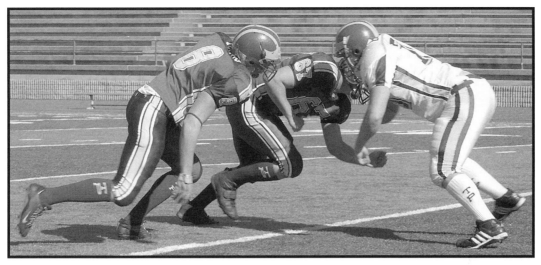

a

b

c

Figure 3.10 Double team block: *(a)* drive blocker and angle blocker both step toward the block; *(b)* blockers are next to each other as they make contact with the defender; *(c)* together they push the defender off the line.

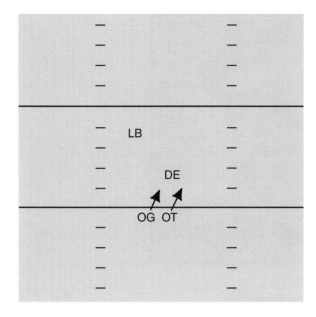

Figure 3.11 Lateral first step with right foot to set up combination block.

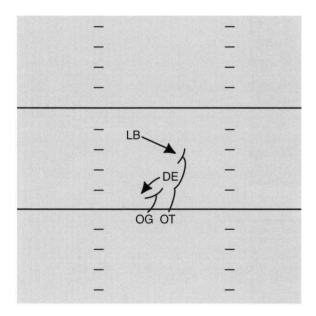

Figure 3.12 Tackle and guard react when the defensive end slants inside during a combination block.

with an attack on the defensive end on the line of scrimmage. The defensive end lines up directly in front of the tackle, while the inside linebacker is in front of the guard off the line of scrimmage (figure 3.11).

On the snap, both the guard and tackle step laterally with their outside foot. On his second step, the tackle strikes the defensive end in the chest with the palm of his inside hand, stopping the tackle's penetration across the line. With his very first step, the guard checks the linebacker in front of him. If he sees the linebacker blitz, the guard must forget the combination block and direct all of his power into blocking the linebacker. When the backer starts to move laterally, on his second step the guard strikes the defensive end with the palm of his outside hand. When both the tackle and guard have made contact with the defensive end, they can drive him off the line and determine if he is playing to the inside or outside of the offensive tackle.

When the defensive end stunts or slants to the inside, the tackle should push the defensive end to the guard after making contact, release to the outside, move up the field, and prepare to block the inside linebacker as he comes behind the defensive end in pursuit (figure 3.12). On an inside stunt by the defensive end, the offensive guard should quickly come around in front of the defensive end, stop his penetration, and keep him from pursuit.

When the defensive end moves to the outside, the guard can help the tackle start to move the defensive end off the line of scrimmage, but he must keep his vision on the linebacker (figure 3.13). If the linebacker starts to move to the outside, the guard must leave the combination block, release inside the defensive end, and use a running drive block on the backer.

Based on the defensive front, players may execute a combination block to the outside or inside, to the left or right. It is important for players to practice against every front with every combination of blockers.

Pull and Drive Block

Another running drive block an offensive lineman needs to learn is the pull and drive block (figure 3.14). Instead of moving straight ahead to block a linebacker, he moves to his left or right down the line of scrimmage to block the defender.

The blocker has to establish a path behind his own offensive linemen. His path starts on the offensive line of scrimmage, but he runs toward the defensive side of the ball when blocking a defensive lineman or linebacker so that he can approach the defensive man from the inside and block him out of the hole. If he is pulling and leading the ball carrier on a wide running play to the outside, he needs to give

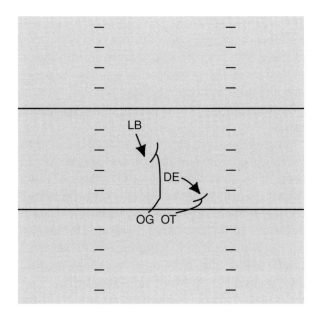

Figure 3.13 Tackle and guard react when the defensive end moves outside.

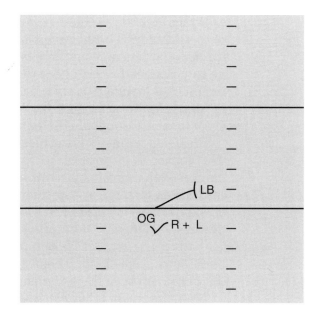

Figure 3.14 Offensive guard pulls right and drive blocks on outside linebacker.

ground away from the line, belly back, and then turn up the field to block a defensive back once he is outside the last block on the line of scrimmage. How far the blocker travels before making contact with the defender depends on his blocking assignment, the play being run, and the defensive player's reaction.

The blocker should practice pulling. For this block, he must immediately change his direction from straight down the field to the left or right on his first step. The first step, a short step with the foot in the direction he will be going, establishes the path he needs to follow to make the block. His path needs to go behind the offensive lineman next to him, so this first step brings him back from his original alignment and starts him in the direction of the block.

To change directions, the blocker takes a short angle step with the foot closest to his new path (figure 3.15). He swings the arm and shoulder that are on the same side as the foot back and around in a quick, hard motion. This motion also brings his upper body around and points his head and shoulders in the direction of the block. With his hand he pushes off the ground and back, and then he shoves off the opposite foot. During this motion, the blocker tries to stay as low as possible.

Once his body is moving down the line, the blocker focuses on the defender he is assigned to block. Depending on the play, the blocker may be asked to block a defensive lineman, a linebacker, or a defensive back.

If he encounters the defender from the side, he should finish the block with the same action as an angle block. As he nears the defender, he

Figure 3.15 Blocker changes directions on the pull and drive block.

explodes with the shoulder pad nearest the line of scrimmage into the exposed side of the defender's body. As his shoulder pad makes contact, he takes the palm of his hand on that side and drives it into the defender's ribs with as much power as he can. His head is in front of the defensive man. From this initial explosion point, the blocker maintains a wide base and continues to drive his legs in short, powerful steps. At the same time, he thrusts his hips forward and down, allowing him to drive up and through the defensive man.

The defender may see the blocker coming and turn to face him. When this occurs, the blocker is in position to make a straight-ahead running drive block. As the blocker prepares to make contact, he bends his knees and lowers his hips slightly. His back is straight, and he keeps his head up and his eyes focused on the center of the defender's chest. The blocker initiates the block with the large muscles of the legs, coming up and through the defender in an explosive motion. The instant his pads make contact, he punches into the numbers of the defender's jersey with both hands. The blocker finishes the block with his legs driving and keeps moving the defender down the line of scrimmage away from the ball carrier's path.

When the player is learning the proper path to run, there is no need for a defender. Once the blocker understands the path, a teammate can play defense while the player goes through each block at half speed. Once he is comfortable with the pull, path, and block, he can increase the speed and go hard against a bag or pad. Finally, the defender reacts to the block, giving the blocker experience similar to what he will see during a game.

Blocking Drills

For each blocking drill, the offensive lineman should begin by working on the first step. Then he should work against a blocking bag. After the blocking bag, the offensive lineman can work against a defensive player at half speed. Finally, he can work against a defensive player at full speed. The defensive player should line up in the proper location for each block. The coach should give the blocker the snap count (first hut) and allow the blocker to get into his stance. Then the coach should start the cadence with the snap count starting movement.

Drive Block

Purpose: To reinforce proper technique for the drive block.

Procedure:

1. Two offensive linemen line up across from each other. One player holds a blocking bag.
2. On the snap, the blocker executes a drive block and drives the blocking dummy 4 yards off the line.
3. Repeat the drill against a defensive player once the blocker learns the proper technique.

Coaching Points: The offensive lineman should maintain a wide base and keep his feet moving, even after contact with the defender. He should keep his elbows close to his ribs as his hands make contact. He should keep his head up and his defender in sight.

Blocking a Linebacker

Purpose: To reinforce proper technique for a drive block on a linebacker who lines up off the line of scrimmage.

Procedure:

1. The linebacker lines up 3 to 4 yards off the line of scrimmage, directly opposite the offensive lineman. The linebacker can use a hand-held blocking dummy at first.
2. The coach calls a running play and gives the blocker the snap count.
3. On the snap, the offensive lineman executes the drive block.
4. The coach should stand behind the blocker and indicate to the linebacker if he should move straight ahead or to the right or left.

Coaching Points: When practicing this block, always call a running play so the blocker knows in which direction the ball will be run. This gives the offensive player a good idea of how to anticipate and adjust to the movement of the defender.

Hook Block

Purpose: To reinforce proper technique for the hook block.

Procedure:

1. The defensive player holds a blocking dummy. He lines up just outside of the blocker's right or left shoulder pad.
2. On the snap count, the blocker executes a hook block and attempts to drive the blocking dummy back 4 yards.
3. The defensive player alternates which side he lines up on. It is important for the blocker to learn to make the hook block in both directions.

Coaching Points: The offensive lineman must use a short, lateral position step followed by a step directly at the defender. The offensive lineman gets into position in front of the defender and drives him back off the line of scrimmage.

Angle Block

Purpose: To reinforce proper technique for the angle block.

Procedure:

1. The defensive player holds a blocking dummy. He lines up in an area that would be in front of the offensive lineman to the blocker's right or left. The player holding the blocking dummy positions himself so that he faces the direction of the block.
2. On the snap count, the blocker executes an angle block and attempts to drive the blocking dummy down the line of scrimmage and back off the line.
3. The defensive player alternates which side he lines up on. It is important for the blocker to learn to make the angle block in both directions.

Coaching Points: The blocker should take a short step down the line with the foot nearest the defender. This first step allows him to get his head in front of the defender and stop him from crossing the line of scrimmage. The second step, taken with his other foot, is his explosion step and allows him to drive the shoulder pad on the same side as this step hard into the side of the defender. Make certain the blocker continues to drive the defender with short, choppy steps.

Double Team Block

Purpose: To reinforce proper technique for the double team block and give players experience from both sides of the double team.

Procedure:
1. In this drill, two offensive blockers work against one defender.
2. The defender lines up directly in front of one of the blockers.
3. On the snap count, the two blockers move in unison to block the single defender.

Coaching Points: On the snap, the blocker directly in front of the defender should execute a drive block, while the offensive blocker to the side should start an angle block. Both blockers should use their shoulder pads and hips together to drive the defensive man back off the line for 4 yards.

Combination Block

Purpose: To reinforce proper technique for the combination block.

Procedure:
1. Two offensive blockers face a defensive lineman and a linebacker. The defensive lineman lines up directly in front of one of the blockers and the linebacker lines up in front of the other.
2. On the snap, the two blockers move in unison against the defensive lineman. Based on the movements of the defensive lineman and linebacker, the blockers separate so that one offensive blocker covers each defender.
3. Once the blockers are in their stances, the coach directs the charge of the defensive lineman and the movement of the linebacker before calling out the snap count.

Coaching Points: When players are first learning the combination block, indicate the direction the defensive end and linebacker will move so the offensive linemen can execute the block versus every charge. When executing the combination block, players should come off low, keep their feet moving, and take short, choppy steps. They should never cross their feet, as this causes them to lose their base and power.

Pull and Drive Block

Purpose: To reinforce proper technique for the pull and drive block.

Procedure:
1. This drill requires two players. The defender can set up at various positions on the defensive line and in the secondary based on the play the coach calls.

2. On the snap, the blocker moves down the line and makes a running drive block on the defender.

Coaching Points: Make certain the blocker takes a short angle step in the direction he will be moving to make the block. He should swing back the arm and shoulder on the same side as his first step so that his body points in the direction of the block. At the same time, he needs to shove off his down hand and opposite foot. The blocker should stay low, shorten his stride, and widen his base as he nears the defender. At contact, his head should be in front of the defender and he should drive his shoulder pad into the defender's side, driving him toward the sideline.

CENTER SNAP

This section focuses on a single position on the offensive line: the center. The center–quarterback exchange is vital to the success of any play.

Center is a demanding and important position on the offensive team. The center and the quarterback are the only two players who touch the ball on every offensive play, and it is the center's initial movement that causes the offensive play to begin. The center must have great skill and be willing to bear tremendous responsibility. However, all offensive linemen should learn to snap the ball so that there is always a player ready to move over in case the center becomes injured.

The coach should face the offensive lineman who is learning to snap and check his stance and grip on the ball. The first step to learning the center snap is an even four-point stance (figure 3.16a). To start, the center gets into the stance with his weight equally distributed on both feet and the fingers of both hands (no ball yet). The center lifts up the hand that he will use to snap the ball to the quarterback (figure 3.16b), and someone puts a ball on the spot where his hand was. The center reaches down and grasps the ball (figure 3.16c).

a   b   c

Figure 3.16 Center stance: *(a)* begin in even four-point stance; *(b)* lift hand used to snap the ball; *(c)* grasp the ball.

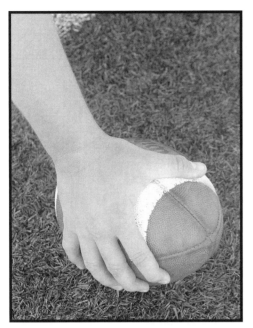

Figure 3.17 Center grasps the ball.

As the center grasps the ball, the laces of the ball are opposite the snapping hand. The palm of the hand is on the outside of the ball. The snapping hand is slightly in front of the ball. The center's fingers are securely under the ball, with his thumb resting over the top of the ball (figure 3.17).

When the center has a good grasp, he is ready to go through the actual snapping motion. The center needs to practice bringing the ball up to the quarterback until they both know they can snap the ball without a fumble. Regardless of his blocking assignment, the center's first responsibility is to snap the ball securely to the quarterback at the proper time. As the center becomes more and more comfortable with the snap, he can move the ball more into the center of his body and lift his other hand off the ground. The next technique the center needs to practice is making the snap while moving as he does when making a block. The center needs to practice moving straight ahead, stepping to the right or left, and dropping straight back in pass protection.

Each center needs to spend time snapping to every quarterback on the team. No one can predict what will happen in a game. The more the center can prepare during practice, the better he will be able to handle whatever situation may come up during a game.

The techniques for making short snaps for extra points and field goals and long snaps for punts are covered in chapter 10, pages 177 and 185. Both types of snaps require special practice and are different from snapping to the quarterback.

Center Snap

Purpose: To fine-tune snapping technique without a ball.

Procedure:

1. At first, players should perform the drill without the ball.

2. The quarterback places his hands in the proper position to take the snap. Another offensive lineman can take his place if the quarterback is unavailable.

3. As the quarterback's hand comes back and up between the center's legs, the center reaches up with his snapping hand and shakes hands with the quarterback's top hand (figure 3.18).

Coaching Points: The center should practice this motion until it is automatic. After the center is comfortable with the motion, add the ball.

Figure 3.18 Center snap drill.

PASS-PROTECTION BLOCKING

There is no bigger challenge for an offensive lineman than protecting the quarterback on a pass play. Every offensive lineman should take great pride in keeping the defense from ever touching the quarterback. For a pass play to be successful, four things must take place:

1. The offensive line must block long enough to give the quarterback the time he needs to deliver the ball.
2. The quarterback must make an accurate throw.
3. The receiver must run a disciplined pass pattern.
4. The receiver must make the catch.

Pass offense starts with the offensive line protecting the quarterback and giving him time to throw. In pass blocking, the offensive lineman's only job is to keep the defensive player from hitting the quarterback before the quarterback has the opportunity to get rid of the ball. Before a pass play, offensive linemen must try to anticipate the direction their defenders will charge during the play and adjust accordingly. Pass protection is an aggressive form of blocking.

The proper stance is very important in pass protection. It is difficult for an offensive lineman to get a good block if his down hand is too far forward. He will have the same problem if he places too much weight on his down hand. When the offensive lineman has to protect the quarterback, he should put just enough weight on his down hand to allow him to push back. The toe of his back foot, the foot on the side of the down hand, should be even with the middle of the other foot. His back should be straight, his shoulders should be square, and his head should be up (figure 3.19).

To move out of his stance, the offensive lineman pushes off his down hand to start his initial movement back off the line of scrimmage. As his shoulders come up, he takes a short step to the inside with his inside foot. This step puts him in position to stop a hard inside charge by the defender (figure 3.20a). Once he takes this step, the offensive lineman bends both knees and lowers his hips. He keeps his back straight and avoids bending forward at the waist. His head is up, and his eyes are focused straight ahead. He brings both elbows in tight against his waist and brings his forearms up so that his hands are in front of his chest. Both hands are up, thumbs together, fingers spread, and palms turned forward.

Figure 3.19 Pass protection stance.

a

Figure 3.20 Pass protection: *(a)* offensive lineman in position to stop defender's charge; *(b)* offensive lineman makes contact with defender.

b

The offensive lineman has to anticipate the direction a defender will charge. During a game, the offensive lineman should watch where the defender lines up. If the defender lines up on the offensive lineman's inside shoulder, he probably will go to the inside. If he is directly in front of the offensive lineman, he can go inside, outside, or attempt to rush right over the offensive lineman. In either situation, the offensive lineman must protect the inside gap first and then react to an outside rush. When the defender lines up on the offensive lineman's outside shoulder, the defender probably will rush outside. Finally, when the defender lines up way outside the offensive lineman, the defender will start to the outside.

Offensive linemen should be able to picture each of these rushes coming at them and react accordingly. Wherever the defender lines up, whether on the inside or outside shoulder or directly in front of the offensive lineman, the offensive lineman should stay square to the line of scrimmage. It is important for the offensive lineman to stay directly in front of the rusher, as he will need to stay between the rusher and the quarterback.

When the offensive lineman sets up in front of the defensive player, his first thought should be to stop the defensive player's momentum. The power to stop the defender starts in the offensive lineman's legs and then comes up through the offensive lineman's body to the palms of both hands. As the defender comes into him, the offensive lineman uses his leg muscles to explode up, avoiding lunging out at the defender. He strikes out aggressively, hitting the defender in the chest with the palms of both hands (figure 3.20b). He pushes forward with both hands to create space between himself and the rusher, and he flexes his knees, lowering his hips. He brings both hands back into his chest and prepares himself to push forward again and again until the pass is thrown or the whistle blows.

When a rusher is definitely going to the offensive lineman's inside or outside, the offensive lineman may not be able to use both hands. In this case, he will have to stop the rusher's momentum by exploding off the leg on the same side as the rush and aggressively hitting into the rusher's chest with the hand on that side. After stopping the rusher, the offensive lineman can try to get more in front of the rusher so that he can use both hands on the second hit. When blocking an outside rusher, the offensive lineman must be careful to not go too far to the outside. If the offensive lineman overextends to the outside, the rusher will quickly change his path and rush inside to the quarterback.

Blocking a defensive rusher who is lined up wide to the offensive lineman's outside requires a change in technique, usually an offensive tackle. The offensive lineman will not be able to stay square to the line of scrimmage. To meet and stop this type of rusher, he must turn his body at a 45-degree angle to the line (figure 3.21).

To get in proper position to block a wide rusher, the offensive lineman should kick his outside foot back and bring his inside foot back and to the outside in a position turned out at a 45-degree angle (figure 3.22). He

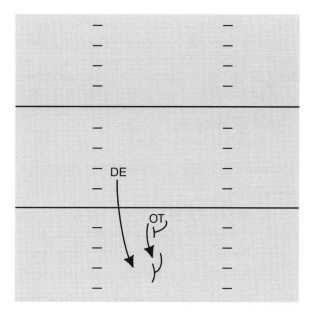

Figure 3.21 Offensive tackle setup against a wide rush by the defensive end.

needs to set up in a good pass protection stance and establish a position directly between the rusher and the quarterback. The offensive lineman must be prepared to meet the pass rusher and use the hand on the same side as the rush to stop the rusher's momentum. After initial contact, the offensive lineman separates, sets again, and stays with the rusher until he hears the whistle.

Figure 3.22   Offensive lineman setting up to block a wide rusher.

Once he is set, the offensive lineman works in a straight line, moving back away from the line as the pass rusher starts to cross his nose. To keep a strong base, the offensive lineman slides his feet as he moves away from the line. He does not cross his feet or bring them too close together, as this weakens his base. By forcing the defender to rush outside, the offensive lineman will always have the opportunity to push him back behind the quarterback.

Pass Protection

Purpose: To reinforce proper pass protection stance and movement after the snap.

Procedure:

1. The coach faces the offensive linemen. At first, no defenders are used and one player goes at a time.
2. The coach gives the snap count and calls out the cadence to start the drill.
3. The offensive lineman gets into the stance for pass protection.
4. When the coach calls the snap, the offensive lineman moves out of the stance and into pass protection.
5. After every offensive lineman is setting up correctly, the coach can have an entire offensive line get into their stance and drop back together. The center can snap the ball to another player acting as the quarterback.

Variation: Once the players are setting up properly, another offensive lineman can line up in front of each blocker to serve as a defensive rush man.

Coaching Points: When the offensive lineman is first learning to pass protect, the defender should rush at half speed. Blockers must stay balanced and not lunge forward to stop the defender. Check that the blockers shuffle their feet and do not cross them during the drill, that they bend at the knees, that their backs are straight and heads are up, and that their hands are in position to strike out at the rusher. Eventually a full-speed pass protection drill can be run with one blocker versus one defensive player at a time. Avoid using more than two offensive blockers in a live drill at one time, because using more than two increases the chance for injury when players run into each other.

Running Back

The running back is in a spotlight position, but he knows that without the blocking of his teammates he would be just another guy out on the field. It is important for the running back to run with great desire, but at the same time he must never forget to give credit to the blockers who open the way for him.

Contact is guaranteed, so the ball carrier must expect to be hit. A beginning running back may feel there isn't any place to run. It may seem to him that he is hit as soon as he touches the ball. He must stay positive, though, because suddenly a hole will open up and he needs to be ready to burst right through it with the ball.

A successful running back possesses certain key skills. This chapter focuses on the stance and start, securing the handoff, receiving passes, evading defenders, and blocking on running and passing plays. Occasionally a running back might have to pass the ball. Check the section on passing on the move in the quarterback chapter (page 32) for the techniques a running back needs to master if he is going to pass the ball.

STANCE AND QUICK START

A running back must be able to move quickly and smoothly once the play begins. He needs to be able to drive straight ahead, move forward at an angle, and move laterally right or left. A functional stance allows the running back to move easily in any direction. The three basic stances used by a running back are the four-, three-, and two-point stances. In each stance, he keeps his feet even, shoulders level, and head up with eyes focused straight ahead. It is important that players not look or lean in the direction they will be running, because either clue helps the defense before the ball is even snapped.

The four-point stance (figure 4.1) allows forward movement with speed and power. To get in the four-point stance, the running back stands with his feet even. He bends his knees so he can rest his forearms on the inner thighs and reaches forward with both arms. He places both hands on the ground slightly in front of his shoulders, making sure his shoulders are even. He keeps his back straight, his head up, and his eyes straight ahead. He stays balanced, never leaning to one side or the other. A fullback who is mainly charging straight ahead, running, and blocking between the offensive tackles uses this stance.

A three-point stance (figure 4.2) allows less speed moving forward, but it makes it much easier to move laterally to the right or left. The running back begins to get into the stance the same way as in the four-point stance. When both forearms are resting on his thighs, the running back reaches out with only one arm. He places very little weight on the fingers of his extended arm as they touch the ground. His down hand is even with his shoulders when the hand reaches the ground. His shoulders are even; he does not lean to the right or left. His back is straight with his weight evenly distributed on the balls of his feet. This is a normal stance that can be used by any running back who is lined up in the backfield because it allows him to move instantly in all directions for any type of play.

Figure 4.1 Four-point stance.

The advantage of a two-point stance (figure 4.3) is it allows the running back to better see the defense. In a two-point stance, the running back gets into his stance as before, but he places both hands on his thighs with his thumbs on the inside. He keeps his head up, looks straight ahead, avoids leaning either way, and keeps his back straight and his weight evenly distributed on both feet. A two-point stance is used by a running back lined up in the backfield in I formation 7 yards off the line and directly behind the quarterback. A running back may also use this stance if he leaves the backfield and lines up wide as a wide receiver before the start of the play.

Starting quickly is one of the greatest abilities a running back can have. After the snap, the running back must instantly be in motion, adjusting his speed based on the blocking pattern or the hole being created.

The first step after the snap is crucial. Regardless of which stance the running back uses, he needs to get moving the instant the ball is snapped. Well-executed footwork is what makes this happen. The first step gets him moving quickly and directs him in a proper path to his running lane. The running back takes his first step with the foot on the side toward which he will be moving (figure 4.4). This is

Figure 4.2 Three-point stance.

Figure 4.3 Two-point stance.

Figure 4.4 Running back's first step.

not a long step; instead it is a short, directional step that sets the body on a path directly toward the attack. If the running back is going to his right, he takes this short directional step with his right foot. If he is going to the left, he steps with his left foot. This is the first step that a running back uses any time he executes a play in which he moves forward toward the line of scrimmage and not laterally toward the sideline.

If a play requires the running back to move laterally, a crossover step is the quickest way for him start after the snap. His first step is with the foot opposite the side of his movement. For example, if he wants to move left, he crosses over with his right foot. After the snap, he leans his body in the direction he wants to go and brings his leg across his body in a natural motion.

The three- or four-point stance can make the crossover step more difficult. To move laterally out of a three- or four-point stance, the running back starts by leaning with his hips in the direction he wants to go (figure 4.5a). He then brings his arm back on the side closest to this direction (figure 4.5b). This arm movement turns his shoulders quickly and opens his hips so that his leg can easily come across (figure 4.5c).

A false step can make the running back arrive late. When a running back is late getting to the hole or to the handoff point, usually it is because he did not get off on the snap or because he had a poor start. Many running backs do not realize that they are taking a false step when they first step back with one foot rather than stepping forward or crossing over. This false step slows their start.

The body and mind become comfortable with what is practiced. It is important for the running back to learn the correct start early in his career. This skill will stay with him as he continues to grow as a running back.

a   b   c

Figure 4.5 Crossover step out of three-point stance: *(a)* running back leans in the direction he wants to go; *(b)* he brings his arm back, turning his shoulders and opening his hips; *(c)* he steps across.

Running Back's Stance

Purpose: To reinforce a functional stance for the running back.

Procedure:

1. Running backs line up in front of the coach.
2. On the coach's signal, the running backs move forward and assume the stances (four-, three-, or two-point) called out by the coach.
3. The coach observes each stance and provides feedback.

Coaching Points: In each stance, make sure the running back's feet are even, his shoulders are level, his head is up, and his eyes are focused straight ahead.

Running Back's Steps

Purpose: To make sure running backs are using the correct stepping technique after the snap.

Procedure:

1. Running backs line up and face the coach.
2. The coach calls out the direction the running backs should step. In the beginning, one player goes at a time.
3. Running backs step in the called direction, and the coach provides feedback on their technique.
4. Players can take three or four steps toward the line after taking the correct directional step.

Coaching Points: Running backs should work on the short, directional step to both the right and left and at different angles to the line of scrimmage.

Crossover Step

Purpose: To reinforce the proper execution of the crossover step.

Procedure:

1. The running back gets into a two-point stance.
2. He leans his shoulders and hips to the right and steps with his left foot.
3. He takes three or four steps toward the sideline after making the crossover step.
4. He lines up in the two-point stance and repeats the drill to the left.
5. He leans his shoulders and hips to the left and steps with his right foot.
6. He takes three or four steps toward the sideline after making the crossover step.

Coaching Points: The coach should make sure the running back is not using a false step before the crossover step. After mastering the crossover step from the two-point stance, the running back should practice the crossover step from the three- and four-point stances.

SECURING THE HANDOFF

Chapter 2 covered the quarterback's responsibility in the handoff; this chapter looks at the running back's job in the handoff. One of the most important skills a running back needs to learn is how to take the ball from the quarterback. All the special skills and ability he may have as a running back will be wasted if he does not take the handoff cleanly. It is the quarterback's job to put the ball firmly to the running back's belly. Once the ball is in the running back's arms, it is his responsibility to secure the ball.

When introducing the running offense, the coach must both show and tell the path he wants the running back to take on each of the various running plays in the offense. It is important for the running back to learn, understand, and practice the exact paths.

The running back and the quarterback must execute the exact footwork to guarantee that they arrive at the handoff point at exactly the same time. If the running back is sloppy in his footwork and path, he will be either too far or too close to the quarterback at the handoff point. When this happens, the handoff will not be clean and may result in a fumble.

Securing the ball is the running back's number-one priority. When he receives the ball from the quarterback, when he is running in heavy traffic, or when he sees that he is going to be hit, the running back needs to make certain that the ball is firmly in his grasp.

During the handoff, the running back forms a pocket with his hands and arms to receive the ball from the quarterback (figure 4.6). One arm is above his belly and one arm is below, creating a pocket for the ball.

It is important that the running back place the upper arm correctly and in the same position every time he takes the handoff. The arm closest to the quarterback is the upper arm. The running back raises his elbow to just below his shoulders so that the forearm is across his chest. He angles the palm of his hand down slightly so that it can quickly engulf the point of the ball.

The position of the lower arm is just as important as that of the upper arm. The arm away from the quarterback forms the bottom of the pocket. The forearm is slightly below and across the running back's belly, and the palm of the hand is turned up.

Once the quarterback puts the ball to the running back's belly, both of the running back's arms grasp the ball (figure 4.7). He quickly lowers his upper hand and forearm and raises his lower hand and forearm, clasping the ball tightly. A beginning running back should keep two arms on the ball to secure it. A more experienced running back can transfer the ball to one arm while running. However, whenever the running back feels that the ball is not secure or when he is about to be hit by more than one tackler, he should not hesitate to get both hands on the ball. Getting the handoff, securing the ball, and protecting it are techniques that must become second nature for the running back.

One technique that will help the running back is visualization. The running back sits quietly with his eyes closed and visualizes taking the handoff for each running play in the offense. He pictures coming to the handoff point and receiving the ball, trying to see in his mind the exact position of his body: the elbow of the near arm is up and the forearm is across the top of his chest; the forearm of his bottom arm is below and across his belly; his head is up and his eyes are focused on the blocking. When taking the handoff, he does not have the luxury of looking at the ball. His vision needs to be on the blocking and the hole that is opening up.

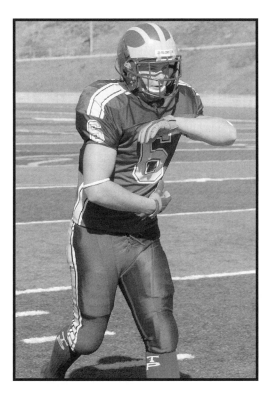

Figure 4.6 The running back creates a pocket for the ball.

Figure 4.7 Running back grasps the ball in both arms.

Taking the Handoff

Purpose: To teach the running back to form a pocket with his arms for the ball.

Procedure:

1. Running backs line up facing the coach. The ball is not used at first.
2. On the coach's signal, the running backs move forward for the handoff.
3. The coach observes the technique of each running back and provides feedback.
4. The quarterback joins in the drill and the actual handoff takes place.

Coaching Points: At the handoff, the running back quickly grasps the ball by raising the bottom hand and forearm and lowering the upper hand and forearm. It is a good idea for beginning running backs to practice running in this position with both hands around the ball. As the running back becomes more experienced, he will know when it is safe to transfer the ball to only one hand.

EVADING TACKLERS

Every running back can improve his running skills by working on certain evasive techniques. It is impossible for a running back to run over defensive players all the time, but there will be times when he has no choice but to secure the ball, lower his shoulders, and drive for as many yards as he can get.

When the opportunity presents itself to make the defensive player miss, the running back should take it. He has the advantage of knowing the direction he is going to cut, while the defensive player can only guess. Two running skills the running back can work on to improve his chances of making the tackler miss are the cutting and crossover techniques. When learning these skills, a running back can use a blocking bag or another running back can act as the defender, standing about 10 yards away.

The running back has to determine which way he is going to cut before starting his forward movement at the defender. When faking to the right, the running back starts the cut with a short step with his right foot to the outside of the defender (figure 4.8a). He needs to quickly move his head and shoulders to the left as his right foot hits the ground. He pushes off his right foot and takes a short change-of-direction step with his left foot (figure 4.8b) that takes him to the outside of the defender (figure 4.8c). He keeps his second step short to keep his feet under his hips. The head and shoulder fake will convince the defender that he is going to the right.

a

b

c

Figure 4.8 Cutting by faking right: *(a)* short step with right foot; *(b)* change of direction step with left foot; *(c)* move continues to the left.

The next technique the running back can use to make a tackler miss is the cross-over step. To use the crossover step, the running back needs to keep space between the defender and himself. When he is 3 to 4 yards away from the defender, the running back starts the move by taking a short step with his right foot to the outside of the defender (figure 4.9a). He takes a second step with his left foot directly at the tackler and makes a quick fake to the right with his head. He then leans his upper body to the left as his left foot hits the ground (figure 4.9b). He quickly brings his right leg completely across his body to change the direction and path of his run (figure 4.9c). Leaning the upper body makes it possible for the running back to bring his leg across his body and make the defender miss.

When a running back has to run toward a sideline, he must do everything he can to make sure the play doesn't create negative yardage. An inside cut technique can help him gain yards. As the running back moves toward the sideline, he must prepare to quickly cut up the field. The running back never wants to be tackled for negative yardage if he can prevent it. He must fake the defender, creating the impression in

a

b

c

Figure 4.9 Crossover step: *(a)* running back executes a short step with his right foot; *(b)* he leans to the left; *(c)* he brings his right leg across.

the defender's mind that he is going to continue to run toward the sideline. Then at the last minute, the running back cuts up the field inside the defender's position for positive yardage.

The running back starts in his normal stance with the ball already in his hands. He rolls over the foot in the direction he is going to run and quickly turns his body toward the sideline (figure 4.10a). As he runs parallel to the line of scrimmage, he picks a point at which the defender will cross the line of scrimmage. He rolls over the foot nearest the line of scrimmage when he is 2 yards from that point and drives up the field as he cuts to the inside (figure 4.10b). A running back first learning this skill should run at half speed at first.

a   b

Figure 4.10   Inside cut: *(a)* running back runs toward sideline; *(b)* he cuts to the inside and drives upfield.

As the running back comes across the formation, he should not angle up toward the line of scrimmage; he should instead sell the defense on the possibility of a wide run. In a game, the running back has a blocker in front of him leading the way (figure 4.11). The running back times his run with his blocker's run, staying slightly behind his blocker. Just as the blocker makes the block on the defensive player, the running back cuts up the field. The running back should practice running behind all the blockers who might block for him. Usually this includes a guard and fullback and possibly a pulling offensive tackle.

Spinning to avoid a defender is a technique that looks spectacular when it works but is very hard to execute properly. When learning this technique, the running back needs the assistance of a coach or another player, who acts as the defensive tackler. The defender's job is to give the running back resistance as he spins.

Beginning running backs who try to spin to avoid being tackled make two common errors: They begin by leaning back with the upper body or they try to execute the spin while too far away from the tackler.

Figure 4.11 Running back times his run with the blocker's run.

When the running back is close enough for the defender to make contact, he steps toward the center of the defender's body with the foot on the same side as his spin (figure 4.12a). If he is spinning to his right, he steps with his right foot. If he is spinning to the left, he steps with his left foot. He must perform this initial step correctly if he is to avoid the grasp of the tackler. When his foot hits the ground, the running back throws his opposite foot, leg, and shoulder around in one smooth motion. For an instant his back is to the tackler as he completes the spin (figure 4.12b). This spin move allows him to quickly move away from the tackler. The instant his leg comes around, he should head upfield once again. If he is to escape from the tackler, he must maintain his speed.

a   b

Figure 4.12 Spin move: *(a)* running back steps to the defender; *(b)* he spins away from the defender.

When the running back practices spinning, he does not have to worry about being hit by a defensive player. In a game, it's different. The running back needs to get into the habit of securing and protecting the ball. If possible, he should have the ball in the hand away from the direction of the spin.

The Cut

Purpose: To reinforce proper cutting technique.

Procedure:

1. The coach lines up as a defender about 10 yards in front of the running back.
2. The running back, with the ball secured, approaches the coach and makes a cut to evade the coach.
3. The coach observes the running back's cut and provides feedback.

Coaching Points: To give the running back a feel for the cut and what it will look like in a game, lean to the side of the running back's first step. He should practice the cut to the left and right. Start the drill at half speed and then have the running back increase the speed of his approach.

Crossover Step

Purpose: To reinforce the proper technique for using a crossover step to elude a defender.

Procedure:

1. The coach lines up as a defender about 10 yards in front of the running back.
2. The running back, with the ball secured, approaches the coach and uses a crossover step to evade the coach.
3. The coach observes the running back's crossover move and provides feedback.

Coaching Points: The running back should practice the crossover move to the left and right. Start the drill at half speed and have the running back increase the speed of his approach. The movement needs to become automatic for the running back, a maneuver he can execute without even thinking about it.

Runs to the Sideline

Purpose: To work on correct technique for running to the sideline to eliminate runs for negative yardage.

Procedure:

1. The coach places a bag to indicate where the running back should cut after running toward the sideline.
2. The running back executes the run toward the sideline, making the cut as indicated.

Coaching Points: The running back should sell the fact that he is going wide to the sideline and not slow down when preparing to cut up the field. Run the drill to both the right and left. Make certain that the running back accelerates up the field for 10 yards once he makes his cut.

Inside Cut

Purpose: To develop the ability to sell the defense on the wide run when making an inside cut.

Procedure:

1. A defensive player sets up opposite a running back with the ball.
2. The defensive player lets the running back get started and then charges across the line to give the running back the feeling of selling the wide run and then cutting up inside.
3. The defensive player can come at the running back from a tight position, from a normal width, or from a wide alignment. The change in width causes the running back to change the point at which he makes his cut up the field.
4. The running back should practice running in both directions.

Variation: Place a shirt or blocking dummy on the ground 2 to 3 yards on the offensive side of the line of scrimmage to mark where the defensive back will be in the game.

Coaching Points: As the running back becomes comfortable with the move, add a quarterback. The quarterback can either hand the ball to the running back or pitch it to him. The running back now has to secure the ball and then locate the point of the defensive man.

Spinning to Get Free

Purpose: To develop proper spinning technique to avoid defenders.

Procedure:

1. The running back starts 5 or 6 yards away from the defender.
2. The defender must push the running back in the chest when the running back is within reach. This contact and push by the defender is similar to what the running back will feel in a game when a tackler begins to make contact.
3. The running back keeps a good forward lean with his upper body all during the drill, especially as contact is made and the running back executes the spin.

Coaching Points: A beginning running back should start at half speed. He can then increase his speed if he is confident he can execute the technique while running at full speed. Emphasize that he should accelerate up the field after completing his spin move.

RECEIVING PASSES

A running back must have the knowledge and techniques necessary to be a part of the passing game. Understanding the fundamentals of the passing game, knowing the importance of timing in pass offense, and perfecting the techniques needed to get open and make the catch are three areas a running back can improve with practice. The running back should know the proper way to catch the ball. He should always try to have both hands and the ball in his vision at the same time when he makes the catch. See chapter 1 for more information on catching technique.

Every receiver must understand the importance of running each pass pattern at the proper depth each and every time. If the running back and quarterback are going to coordinate the passing game, the running back must make certain that he plays his part correctly. When first learning pass routes, the running back should practice without a quarterback and run all pass routes at half speed. Once he has a feel for how to run the different routes correctly, he can run them at full speed.

Three Zones

The running back must first understand the different depths of his various pass patterns. The distance he runs down the field is coordinated with the number of steps the quarterback takes in his drop, the time the offensive line has to pass block and protect the quarterback, and the manner of the pass-protection blocking. By running his pattern at the proper depth, he helps ensure the correct timing of the pass. The running back should think of the field as being divided into three separate depths or zones: short, medium, and deep.

The short zone extends from the line of scrimmage to 6 yards up the field. Patterns run in this area will be quick. The quarterback may drop three or five steps before delivering the ball. The timing must be exact. The running back will not have time to make elaborate moves; he must run quickly up the field, break sharply into his pattern, and immediately look for the ball.

The medium zone starts at 7 yards past the line of scrimmage and goes up to 12 yards. In this zone the running back has the opportunity to get open. Patterns will often be continuous movement routes in which he keeps running before getting the ball. To pass to this zone, the quarterback uses a five-step drop. The offensive linemen know they must protect for a longer time.

The deep zone extends from the medium zone all the way to the opponent's goal line. Patterns in this area require more time and often the running back has to run under the ball. The quarterback uses a seven-step drop and should lead the running back, giving him the opportunity to separate from the defender and make the reception.

It is important for the running back to be able to recognize the different zones as he is on the move. One of the best ways to get a feel for the different depths is to take time every day to run up the field calling out the zone he is in or mentally saying to himself, "Short, short, short," "Medium, medium, medium," and "Deep, deep, deep," as he travels up the field.

Learning Pass Routes

Once the running back has an understanding of the depths of each zone, he is ready to learn the different pass routes that he will run in each zone. Learning to run the pass patterns or routes is something running backs can practice on their own. In fact, it is good for a running back to practice without a quarterback or ball. When practicing different routes, the running back should concentrate on releasing quickly, running the routes at the proper depth, breaking at the proper point, getting his head around quickly to see the ball and the quarterback, having his hands in proper position for the catch, and running the route to completion.

Short Pass Routes. In the short zone, the most important thing for the running back to remember is to look quickly for the ball. There are three basic pass patterns in the short zone: flat, angle, and wide (figure 4.13). The quarterback might take only a three-step drop before throwing the ball to the primary receiver. If the quarterback drops only three steps, the offensive line will block aggressively and the quarterback will throw the pass very quickly.

It is important that these three pass patterns be timed correctly. The running back must take the responsibility for getting off quickly on the snap count, running hard, breaking at the proper depth, and looking for the ball as soon as possible. Because the running back's initial alignment usually is 4 yards behind the line of scrimmage, he cannot go very far upfield before he makes his break.

In the flat pattern, the running back attacks the line of scrimmage at a 45-degree angle just outside of his offensive tackle. Once he has gone 1 yard across the line of scrimmage, he rolls over his outside foot and breaks directly toward the sideline. As he continues to run to the outside of the field, he turns his head back toward the quarterback and he looks for the ball. He must expect the pass at any height. Many times the ball will be low and in front and he will have to adjust his path to make the catch.

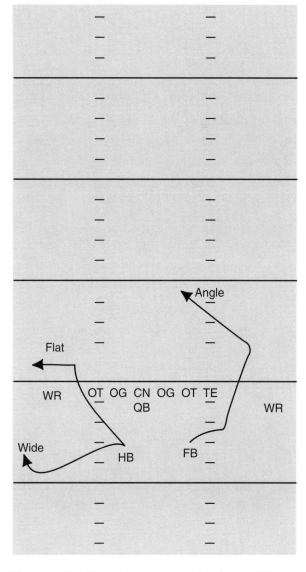

Figure 4.13 Three short pass routes for the RB: flat, angle, and wide.

When running the angle pattern, the running back starts out exactly as he would if he were going to run a flat route. When he is 1 yard across the line of scrimmage, instead of breaking to the sideline he breaks at a 45-degree angle back into the center of the field. He turns his head back to the quarterback the second he makes his break and tries to pick out the ball the instant it leaves the quarterback's hand. In this pattern, the ball travels a short distance and gets to the running back very quickly. He must locate the ball and make the catch the instant he turns back to the center of the field. He should have his hands ready to reach out for the ball.

The wide pattern also is run to the outside of the field. It is run on the offensive side of the line of scrimmage. The running back starts with a crossover step with his inside foot as he begins to run the route. Because the quarterback will be even with the running back or even slightly in front of him, it is essential that the running back angle slightly away from the line of scrimmage with his first few steps. This allows him to see the ball better and, more important, it allows him to be turned up the field when he makes the catch. On a wide pattern, the quarterback throws the

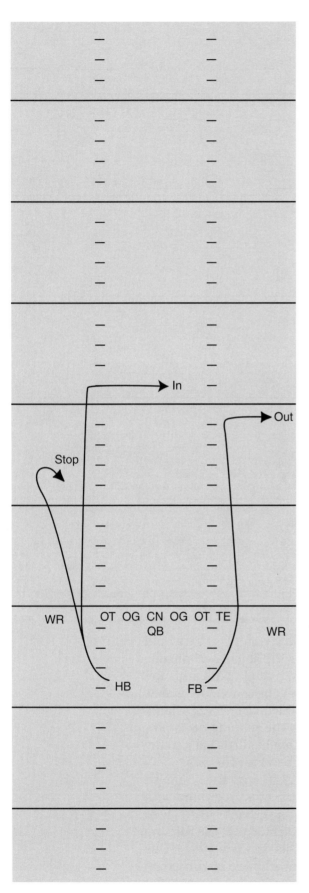

ball in front of the running back. The quarterback is going to expect the running back to be turned up the field and running under the pass. If the quarterback is in front of the running back and the running back senses the pass will be incomplete, he needs to be sure to cover up the ball. Otherwise the pass may be ruled a lateral, which could be recovered by the defense.

The receiver must expect to be tackled the minute he touches the ball, especially on short pass routes. It is important for the running back to secure the ball the instant it is in his hands. If the hit doesn't happen immediately, so much the better, but at least the running back is prepared for it.

Medium Pass Routes.   A medium receiver operates in an area 7 to 10 yards across the line of scrimmage. For a running back, this means he has to run 11 to 15 yards before making his final break to catch the ball on any medium pass route.

Because of the distance that must be covered on any medium route, speed is the running back's greatest asset. He cannot afford to come out at half or three-quarter speed. The quarterback will not have time to wait for the running back to make his break. It is also important for defenders to get the impression that the running back may be going deep.

Running any pass pattern starts with a good release from the presnap position in the backfield. The running back should try to make the release of all medium or deep routes look the same to the defense. Both the in and out pass patterns are run this way (figure 4.14). The one exception is a stop route, which calls for an angle release and is run at 7 yards.

For the out and in pass patterns, the running back's release should be just wide enough to guarantee that he will clear any offensive blocker or defensive rush man. Once he sees that he is clear to the outside, he must immediately turn up the field and make the defense think he is going deep on his pass route.

On the out route, the running back rolls over his outside foot at 9 yards and breaks directly for the sideline. When the quarterback throws the ball, the running back may need to come back toward the line of scrimmage to make the catch. When catching the pass, the running back turns his shoulders, heads back to the quarterback, and reaches back with both hands to make the catch.

Figure 4.14   Three medium pass routes for the RB: in, out, and stop.

The in route is run off the same release as the out route. The running back runs up the field 10 yards past the line of scrimmage, rolls over his inside foot, and breaks across the center of the field. The minute he breaks, his head turns back to the quarterback. He is ready to turn his shoulders to the line to get both hands in position to make the catch. For proper timing, the running back must keep running at full speed after the break.

When running a stop route, the running back must locate the spot where he will make his final cut before the snap of the ball. He must try to run a straight line to that spot. The initial target spot in a stop pattern is 7 yards across the line of scrimmage and 8 yards outside of where the offensive tackle lined up. When the running back nears this spot, he must gather himself and prepare to turn to either the inside or outside away from the nearest defensive coverage man. He turns his head back to the quarterback the instant he makes his stop. He brings both hands up and prepares to make the catch. The quicker the quarterback can get the ball to the running back, the sooner the running back can make the catch, put the ball away, and run up the field.

Deep Pass Routes. A running back probably will have only two or three chances to run a deep pass pattern during a game. These pass routes take more time—the quarterback needs to hold the ball longer, and the offensive line has to block longer before the ball is thrown. Deep patterns open up when the running back has successfully caught passes in the short and medium zones. Because there are so few chances of catching a deep pass, it is essential for the running back to run his route correctly, run at full speed, get open, and make the reception.

When a running back runs a deep pattern—a flat and up, seam, post, or fan route (figure 4.15)—it helps if the defender thinks he is running a short or medium route. If the running back can get the defender to commit to a short or medium pattern, the running back can break clear and get in position to make a catch for a long gain.

For the flat and up pattern, the running back should look back for the ball as he runs to the sideline. When he is about 6 yards from the sideline, he rolls over the foot nearest the defense and turns and runs straight up the field. He turns his head back to the inside and focuses on the quarterback, expecting the pass to be lofted to him. He runs under the pass and makes the catch.

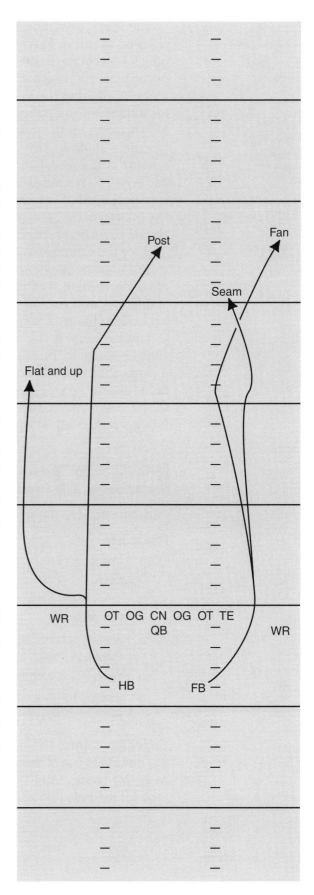

Figure 4.15 Four deep pass routes for the RB: flat and up, seam, post, and fan.

The seam, post, and fan pass patterns start exactly as if the running back were running an out or in route in the medium zone. When the defender thinks the running back is going to break either to the outside or inside, he will slow his coverage, putting the running back in great position to run by him.

When running the seam route, the player starts up the field just like he would for a medium route. Instead of breaking for the out or in route, he continues running straight up the field. At 12 yards past the line of scrimmage, the running back begins to angle slightly to the inside. As he runs the seam pattern, he stays on the outside of the hash marks. This is one deep pass pattern in which the pass may be drilled to the running back, and not lofted. Because the ball may get there quickly, it is important that the running back quickly turn his head to the inside and focus on the quarterback. Ideally the ball will come over the running back's inside shoulder, but he must be prepared for it to come directly over his head or to the outside.

Once the running back has learned to run the seam pattern correctly, he can begin to work on the post pattern. Everything is the same as the seam route except that at 14 yards instead of running straight up the field the running back rolls over his inside foot and runs at a deep angle to the center of the field. He looks back over his inside shoulder and expects to run under the pass.

The fan route is the most difficult to complete. At 8 yards, as the running back runs up the field, he angles slightly to the inside of the field. When he has run 2 or 3 yards at an angle, he rolls over his outside foot and breaks at a deep angle up the field toward the sideline. He turns his head over his outside shoulder to look back to the quarterback. He looks for the ball to be lofted over his outside shoulder and is prepared to adjust his path to the path of the ball.

Running Pass Routes

Purpose: To give the running back experience running different pass routes.

Procedure:

1. The coach lines up in the quarterback's setup position and faces the running back.
2. The coach calls out the pass route and the running back gets into position for the play.
3. The coach begins the play by calling out the snap and the running back runs the pass route.
4. The coach offers feedback on the running back's performance.
5. In the beginning keep the ball out of the drill. Once players can correctly run each route, add a quarterback and the ball.

Coaching Points: The running back must start immediately on the snap. Check that the pattern is run at the correct depth, that the running back does not slow down to make his break, and that he turns his head back at the earliest possible moment to look for the ball. Run all the patterns to both the right and left.

BLOCKING

All good running backs can run with the ball. Great running backs are also good pass receivers when coming out of the backfield. Exceptional running backs excel at running and catching and have the ability and desire to be great blockers. The combination of these three skills makes the complete running back.

A running back needs to block on running plays when his backfield partner is carrying the ball. On pass plays, he may become part of the pass protection blocking for the quarterback. It is important for a running back to become skilled in both types of blocking.

Blocking for Running Plays

For running plays, the running back needs to understand that the quicker he can get to the defender the better. He blocks only one side of the defender (figure 4.16). He shortens his stride as he nears the defender. His shoulders are slightly in front of his hips, and his hips are over his feet. He bends his knees, he makes contact with the shoulder and forearm at the defender's hip, and he keeps his legs driving even after contact. The contact point is at the defender's hip on the side opposite the direction the running back wants to block the defender. The running back's head slides to the outside of the defensive man's hip. He explodes off the foot on the same side as his block.

A running back may block a linebacker who is lined up on the end of the line or at an inside position. In either situation, the block is at the point of attack, where the ball is being run, and it is crucial to the success of the play. In both instances, the running back must take the most direct route to the linebacker. The quicker he gets to the linebacker, the less time the linebacker has to react and set

Figure 4.16 Blocking for a running play.

himself to defeat the block. The running back should practice taking the same path directly toward the linebacker, not changing his path when he blocks the defender in or out.

The running back may be asked to block an outside linebacker to the inside on wide running plays or to the outside on off tackle plays. The path to the linebacker on both blocks should be the same. This is the same blocking that can be used if the running back blocks a defensive back coming up on the outside. The difference between the two blocks is the running back's target area. If the running back is blocking the linebacker to the outside, the running back hits the linebacker's inside hip area. If the running back is blocking the linebacker to the inside, he contacts the linebacker's outside hip. The running back must focus on the target area and make good contact with his shoulder pad and forearm.

When blocking the linebacker to the outside, the running back should explode off his outside foot and make contact with the linebacker's inside hip with his outside shoulder pad and forearm. He should allow his head to slide along the side of the backer. The running back then drives the linebacker back and to the outside of his original position.

When the running back blocks the outside linebacker to the inside, his path is the same, except now he aims for the outside linebacker's outside hip. His explosion to start the block comes off his inside foot. He makes contact with the linebacker's outside hip with his inside shoulder pad and forearm. Once the running back makes his hit, his goal is to drive the backer back toward the center of the field.

If the play calls for the running back to block an inside linebacker away from the center or back toward the center, the running back can use the same technique as when blocking an outside linebacker.

The running back may lead block on an inside linebacker. In this type of play, the ball carrier cuts off (goes opposite) his block. The running back does not know at the start of the play which direction he is going to block the linebacker. The running back should focus on the linebacker's numbers, take a path directly at the linebacker, allow the linebacker to choose a side, and then block the linebacker. The technique for the block is the same. The running back has to be ready to quickly decide which side of his body he is going to use to block and which of the defender's hips he is going to attack.

Blocking for Pass Plays

When blocking for the quarterback on pass plays, the running back is unable to attack the defender as he did on a run block. Now he must position himself and wait for the defender to rush at him.

Most of the time, the running back needs to block a defender, usually a linebacker or defensive back, who is rushing the quarterback from the outside. There may be times when he blocks an inside linebacker who is rushing on the inside.

Often on a pass block, the running back is unable to stop the defender in his tracks. If the running back knows where the quarterback is setting up, it is much easier to use the defender's momentum and block him past the quarterback. It is the running back's responsibility to know how deep the quarterback is going to drop and where he will finally set up to deliver the pass.

To be the best pass blocker there are some basic points that the running back should know. The running back needs to position his body between the pass rusher and the quarterback (figure 4.17). He keeps his feet parallel and slightly wider than shoulder-width apart. He flexes his knees, keeps his back straight, and keeps his head up and his eyes focused straight ahead. Both elbows are belt-high and close to the side of the running back's body. He bends his elbows so that his forearms come up in front

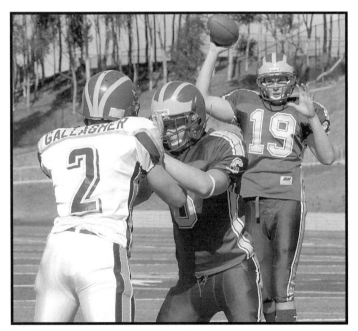

Figure 4.17 Blocking on a pass play.

of his numbers. Both hands are in front of his jersey, palms up, fingers open. He explodes with his legs and hits aggressively when contact occurs.

One easy way to practice setting up properly is to put a shirt or towel on the ground 7 yards from the line of scrimmage, where the quarterback will be when he is going to pass the ball. The running back lines up to the right or left of this position in the same place he would be when lining up in the backfield. From his normal stance, he can set up to block an outside rusher and an inside rusher.

When he sets up to block an outside rusher, the running back takes a step forward and in with his inside foot. He swings his outside leg and foot back to end up with both feet even, shoulders square. His body is turned directly toward the sideline in a blocking position.

With his body turned directly toward the sideline, the running back gives the defender only one way to rush—up the field. When the rusher is close, the running back must slow his rush by hitting the center of his chest aggressively with the palm of the hand that is away from the line of scrimmage. He can use the palm of the other hand to hit into the rusher's shoulder and assist in pushing him upfield past the quarterback. Once the running back makes contact, he needs to keep shuffling his feet, staying between the rusher and the quarterback.

Blocking an inside rusher starts the same way, with a good inside and forward step with the running back's inside foot. He then steps up with his outside foot, evens his stance, and looks directly upfield.

When pass blocking an inside pass rusher, the running back sets up to end up inside of the rusher. The running back wants to block him to the outside and direct him past the quarterback. The running back focuses on the rusher's chest. As the rusher nears, the running back bends his knees and prepares to strike him in the chest with the palms of both hands. Once he makes contact and stops the rusher, he extends his arms and creates some space between the defender and himself. As he creates this space, he shuffles his feet, brings his arms and hands back to their set position, and once again gets between the rusher and the quarterback. During a game, he should continue this hitting and separating until he has driven the rusher past the quarterback, the pass is thrown, or the whistle blows.

The hardest pass block comes when an inside rusher is determined to rush up the middle, inside the running back's position. The running back must be certain that the defensive man is really rushing to his inside and not trying to fake him so that he can go past the running back to the outside. When the running back sees the defender's chest cross his nose, he can be fairly sure that the rusher is trying to rush up the middle, not to the outside. When he sees the rusher in this position, he steps back slightly with his inside foot and pushes off his inside leg. He strikes the rusher in the chest with the palm of his inside hand and steps quickly with his outside foot toward the defender. He then hits out with the palm of his other hand and drives the rusher across the field.

A running back who is a good pass protection blocker allows the team to run plays from the blocking action. These plays make the defense think the running back is blocking to protect the quarterback, but then the running back becomes either the ball carrier or the primary receiver. Success with these plays is based on how well the running back pass blocks.

The draw play (figure 4.18), in which the offense sells the pass and then runs the ball, is a great play especially against teams that are trying to rush the passer. On a draw play, the offensive line sets up to pass block, the quarterback drops back as if to pass, and the running back steps inside as if he is going to block an inside pass

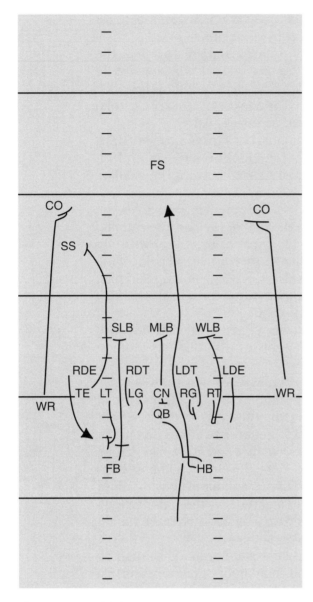

Figure 4.18 HB draw.

rusher. The defense sees the play start as if it were a drop-back pass. When all three segments of the offensive team are working together, some of the defensive players will start rushing hard up the field while others will drop back into coverage.

The running back's role in the draw play is very important. He moves to the inside to be in position for the quarterback to easily hand him the ball. When the ball is snapped, the running back steps laterally to the inside with his inside foot and bring his outside foot to the inside so that he has a balanced stance. He bends his knees and keeps his back straight, his head up, and his eyes focused on the offensive line. He positions his arms as if he were taking a hand-off. The running back lets the quarterback put the ball to his belly and then secures the ball. He immediately starts upfield through any hole that opens up.

For the delay route (figure 4.19), the running back steps to the inside and sets up just as he would for an inside pass-protection assignment. As he sets up, the quarterback drops back to pass, the offensive line blocks to protect the quarterback, and ideally the defensive line-backers drop off the line to help on pass coverage. As he sets up in his blocking position, the running back mentally counts, "A thousand one, a thousand two, a thousand three." Then he runs downfield between the offensive tackle and guard blocks. Once he crosses the line of scrimmage, he angles back to the center of the field and turns his head to the inside to find the quarterback. He expects the ball to arrive immediately, 3 to 4 yards downfield. After catching the ball, he secures it and turns upfield, anticipating contact from the linebackers.

The third type of play from the pass blocking position is the screen pass (figure 4.20). Once again the running back sets up in the inside pass blocking position. Just like the delay pattern, a screen pass requires enough time for the offensive lineman to block the pass rushers and then move to the outside to block for the running back. As he sets up, the running back counts to a thousand three. He then takes one or two short steps up the line of scrimmage, releases behind the block of his offensive tackle, and moves to the outside. He turns his head back toward the quarterback and looks for the ball. The pass should come over the shoulder farthest from the line of scrimmage. After securing the ball, he yells "Go!" or another word to alert his offensive blockers that he has the ball.

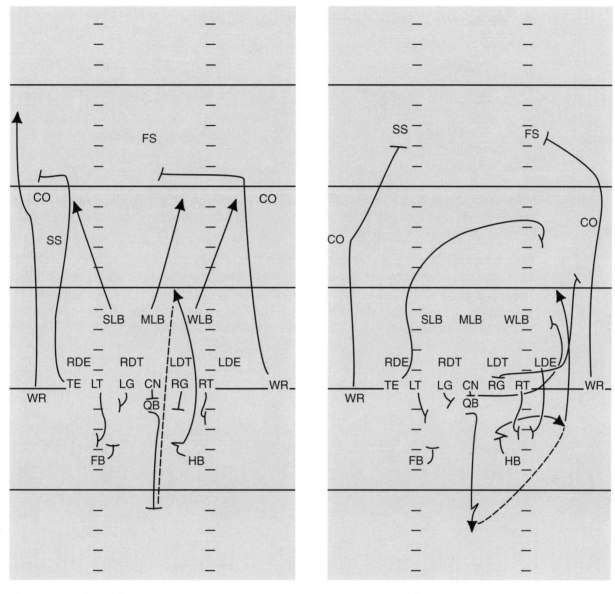

Figure 4.19 HB delay.

Figure 4.20 HB screen right.

When setting up a screen pattern, the running back must stay alert for any blitzing linebacker. If the running back sees that the linebacker is rushing, he should step up and deliver a hit on the backer, stopping his free rush to the quarterback. After the first hit on the linebacker, he can let him go and start moving to the outside on the pass pattern.

The draw, delay, and screen are plays that the running back can practice on his own. Since the setup is the same for all three plays, they can be mentally called and then executed. A running back needs to practice these movements on his own so they become automatic for him.

Blocking the Outside Linebacker

Purpose: To develop blocking ability on an outside linebacker.

Procedure:

1. The coach or another back lines up in the defender's position and holds a hand dummy to the side of the block.
2. The running back sets up in position. On the coach's signal, the running back approaches the dummy to block it.
3. The coach tells the running back which side to block.

Variation: This drill is also good for practicing blocking on an inside linebacker. The coach or another running back lines up as an inside linebacker, and the coach calls out the direction of the block.

Coaching Points: The blocker should take the same path at the defender whether he is blocking him in or out. When blocking a linebacker to the outside, the blocker should take off with his outside foot and make contact on the backer's inside hip with his outside shoulder pad. The opposite is true when blocking the backer to the inside. Have the blocker drive the backer for 4 yards after contact.

5

Wide Receiver

One play by a wide receiver can quickly change the outcome of the game, but consistency is the most important characteristic of a good receiver. Every wide receiver needs to be able to catch the ball. The position also requires the physical skills to get open and a great deal of work to become truly skilled. Good receivers run more and work harder than anyone else on the offense and they believe they can catch every ball thrown to them.

Some of the challenges the wide receiver faces are difficulty shedding the defensive player, going one way then seeing the ball thrown in another direction, having a ball fly through his hands and land on the ground, and being hit while making the catch. Each of these situations has happened to every wide receiver. Staying positive and not becoming discouraged is important.

This chapter focuses on the techniques and skills a top wide receiver needs: stance and release, pass routes and timing, and blocking.

STANCE AND RELEASE

Often wide receivers move straight across the line of scrimmage as play begins. Speed and quickness when the ball is snapped are essential for success. Their beginning stance must allow for quick forward movement. Which stance to use depends on the team's style of offense. For most offenses, either a three-point stance or an upright two-point stance is appropriate.

In the three-point stance (figure 5.1), the wide receiver starts by standing up with his feet even and hip-width apart. The receiver keeps his back straight and his knees bent, resting both forearms on the inner thighs. From this position, the player reaches out with the hand nearest the sideline and steps back with the foot on that side of his body. Keeping his back straight and his head up, he turns his head slightly inside to see the ball when it is snapped. The receiver should be on the balls of both feet, placing more weight on the front foot. This allows him to

Figure 5.1 Three-point stance.

step with the back foot, rolling over the front foot as he moves forward. The hand touching the ground is slightly ahead and slightly to the outside of the front of his shoulders. The back foot is slightly behind the heel of the front foot.

An upright two-point stance (figure 5.2) starts with the feet even and hip-width apart. From this position, the player steps back with his inside foot so that it is three to four inches behind his front foot. He adjusts his weight to the front foot, keeping only the toe of his back foot on the ground to maintain balance. The receiver bends forward slightly at the waist as he steps back. He allows his head and shoulders to move in front of his feet and hips. His arms and hands hang down naturally or he raises his elbows and forearms to get into more of a running stance. He turns his head slightly to the inside to see the ball being snapped. He begins his forward movement by quickly stepping forward with the back foot. When leaning forward, the receiver is careful not to go offside.

A wide receiver who can instantly attack the defensive back has a great advantage. Whether he uses an upright two-point stance or a three-point stance with one hand on the ground, the ability to get an instant start is crucial. A wide receiver should release with the same intensity and quickness on every play, whether it is a running play or a passing play. The receiver should not let the defensive player know when he is the primary receiver or when the ball is being run to his side.

When attacking the defender, the receiver's goal is to quickly narrow the distance between himself and the defensive back. He wants the defensive back to turn and begin to run deep. The wide receiver will be able to execute his pass pattern and make the catch when the defensive back is turned and running deep.

Figure 5.2 Two-point stance.

Releasing from tight coverage requires skill. When faced with a defender directly in front of the receiver on the scrimmage line, the receiver must adjust his stance. Against this type of press coverage, the receiver places his back foot forward but angled away from the defender instead of stepping straight up with the back foot (figure 5.3a). This creates a small space in which to work. He now has the opportunity to bring the arm closest to the defensive back up past his shoulder (figure 5.3b). This ripping-up motion is usually enough to get the defensive man's hand off his jersey (figure 5.3c).

a

b

c

Figure 5.3 Releasing from tight coverage: *(a)* the wide receiver steps away from the defender; *(b)* the defender makes contact; *(c)* the wide receiver raises his arm to swat the defender's hand away.

A wide receiver has trouble getting open when he comes off the ball late. The receiver should not step back with his front foot on a release. When the defensive back lines up right in front of him, the wide receiver should drive off the line and not spend time moving only his head and shoulders.

RUNNING PASS ROUTES

Every wide receiver must understand the importance of running each pass pattern at the proper depth each and every time. If the receiver and the quarterback are going to coordinate the passing game, the receiver has to take care of his part. On every pass play, the wide receiver is responsible for running the route at the proper depth and in the correct manner and then catching the ball. The quarterback is responsible for getting the ball to the receiver where the receiver can make the catch. The offensive line and, on occasion, the offensive backs assume the responsibility of blocking the defensive players long enough to give the quarterback time to make the pass. It is a coordinated effort that must occur in order for the pass to be thrown and caught; for success, everyone must do his job.

First, the receiver needs to learn the different depths at which to run the pass patterns. Three actions determine the distance he runs down the field:

1. The number of steps the quarterback takes in his drop.
2. The time the offensive line needs to protect the quarterback.
3. The type of blocking used by the offensive line.

Running the pattern at the proper depth helps ensure correct timing of the pass. Think of the field as being divided into three separate depths or zones: short, medium, and deep.

The short zone extends from the line of scrimmage up the field for 6 yards. Patterns run in this zone are quick. The quarterback drops only three steps before delivering the ball. The timing in this area must be exact. The wide receiver must run quickly up the field, break sharply into his pattern, and immediately look for the ball.

The medium zone starts at 7 yards and goes up to 15 yards. In this zone, the receiver can use all his moves to get open. Medium patterns are often continuous-movement routes in which the receiver keeps running before he gets the ball. In this zone, the quarterback uses a five-step drop and the offensive line knows that they must protect for a longer time.

The deep zone extends from the far edge of the medium zone all the way to the opponent's goal line. The patterns run in this zone require more time and often the receiver has to run under the ball. The quarterback tries to give the receiver the opportunity to separate from the defender and make the reception.

It is important for a receiver to be able to recognize the different zones when on the move. One way to get a feel for the different depths is to take time every day to run up the field calling out the zone or mentally saying, "Short, short, short," "Medium, medium, medium," and "Deep, deep, deep" while traveling up the field. Once the receiver has an understanding of the depths for each zone, he is ready to learn the different pass routes he will run in each zone.

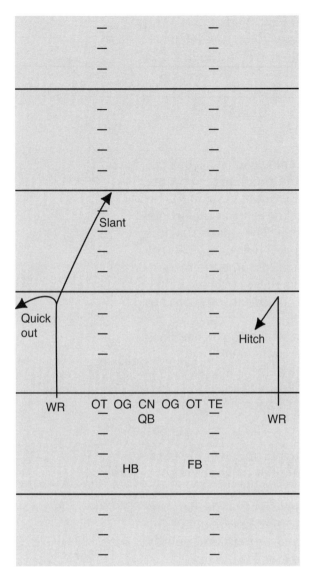

Figure 5.4 Short routes for the wide receiver: quick out, hitch, and slant.

Short Routes

The team often goes to the short passing game to get the passing attack started. The short passing game can quickly move the ball, neutralize a blitzing defense, and allow the quarterback to get into a passing rhythm.

Because the quarterback takes only a three-step drop before throwing the ball, timing is the number-one priority for the short passing game. The wide receiver's contribution to the timing of the short passing game involves three factors. First, he must run each of the short patterns at the proper depth, making it possible for the wide receiver and the quarterback to properly time the pass. Second, every short route must be run at a constant speed, and they must be run at full speed. Any slowing down on the break or coming out of the break usually results in an incomplete pass. Third, the receiver must be prepared to catch the ball immediately. The receiver has to turn his head and focus his eyes on the quarterback the instant he makes his break. Mentally he prepares to position his hands to make the catch. The three major short pass routes are the quick out, the hitch, and the slant (figure 5.4). Each is run differently but involves these three factors.

Quick Out. When running a quick out pass pattern, the receiver must drive hard off the line to sell the defensive back on the idea that he is going deep. At 4 yards, the wide receiver rolls over his outside foot and redirects his momentum toward the sideline. The receiver probably will run 6 or 7 yards before the pass arrives.

As he runs toward the sideline, the receiver needs to be prepared to come back toward the original line of scrimmage to make the catch. He should expect the pass to be low, which often occurs when the quarterback throws at such a sharp angle to the outside. The receiver should have his hands below his waist with his little fingers together to form the catching pocket (figure 5.5).

Hitch. The hitch pattern is more difficult. The receiver's momentum has to completely stop and he has to come back for the ball. He wants to run full speed to sell the defensive back on the idea that he is going deep. At 5 yards, he plants his outside foot to stop his forward movement. Once he plants his outside foot, he sits back slightly and turns his body back to the inside to face the quarterback. Because the ball should be there almost as he turns, he must have his hands even with his numbers and his thumbs together, ready to make the catch.

Slant. The third short pass pattern is the slant pass. During the slant route, the receiver redirects his upfield run. Again, he comes off the line of scrimmage at full speed. When he reaches 4 yards, he rolls over his inside foot and redirects his momentum, running at a 45-degree angle into the center of the field. When running a slant route, the receiver expects the quarterback to lead him, so he runs up the field 6 or 7

Figure 5.5 Wide receiver's hands in position to catch a low pass.

yards before the ball arrives. The slant pass can arrive at any height, so the receiver must be ready to position his hands quickly to make the catch. His head and eyes must turn to the quarterback the instant he starts his move to the inside.

On all three short pass routes, the receiver must prepare to be hit immediately. He should concentrate first on making the catch and securing the ball. Running with the ball comes after doing those two things.

Basic Medium Routes

It is essential for any good wide receiver to learn and master the proper techniques for running medium pass routes. While running these patterns, the receiver positions the defensive back by altering the path the receiver takes as he moves up the field.

There are three basic medium pass routes: hook, in, and out (figure 5.6). All three have a 10- to 12-yard breaking point. On these passes, the quarterback uses a five-step drop to move away from the line of scrimmage. If the receiver runs at full speed, the receiver and the quarterback should be able to time the pass correctly.

Hook.   When running the hook, the wide receiver must make the defensive back believe that the receiver is going deep. The receiver comes off the line in a full sprint straight up the field, forcing the defensive back to turn and run at full speed toward his own goal line. As the receiver nears the 12-yard area, he lowers his hips slightly and stops his momentum by stepping with his outside foot. He quickly turns his body to the inside and faces the quarterback when his outside foot hits the ground.

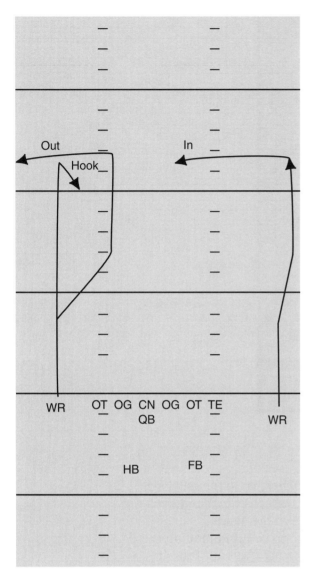

Figure 5.6 Basic medium pass routes for the wide receiver: hook, in, and out.

When playing on a wet or slick surface, the receiver can stop his momentum by taking three quick steps, allowing him to keep his feet under his hips at all times.

In the hook pattern, the ball may be on the way as the receiver turns back to the inside. His hands must be up, his chest high, his eyes looking for the ball. If the quarterback is late, the wide receiver should continue moving back toward the ball.

Out and In Patterns. The out and in pass patterns are run identically. The in pattern goes toward the center of the field, and the out pattern goes toward the sideline. Both pass patterns start with a hard drive straight up the field. During this drive, the receiver needs to see where the defender is in relation to where the receiver wants to go. If the defender is where the receiver wants to go, the receiver should angle in the opposite direction and take the defensive back out of the area. If the defensive back is opposite where the receiver's pattern will take him, the wide receiver should drive at an angle directly toward the defender and make him move farther away from the receiver's final cut.

After relocating the defensive player, the receiver sprints straight up the field again and sells the fact that he is going deep. As he nears the 12-yard area, the receiver prepares to make his final cut into the pattern.

Both of these pass routes must be run at full speed. The receiver has to roll over the foot in the direction he is headed and not stop his momentum. If he is going to his outside on an out route, he leans his upper body to the outside and rolls over his outside foot. For an in pattern, he leans his upper body to the inside and rolls over his inside foot.

Using this technique to run these pass routes may cause the player to round the pattern off, but he will be going at full speed. As he takes the second step to the inside or the outside, he may have to adjust his pass route slightly back toward the line of scrimmage. This adjustment gives him a chance for greater separation from the defender, plus it brings him back toward the ball and decreases the chance of an interception. A slight adjustment back toward the line of scrimmage is especially important on an out route, as the quarterback throws the ball a greater distance than on an in route.

The receiver must keep coming across the field on the in route, as the quarterback may come to him late. He should make certain that he is at least 12 yards from the sideline when he breaks in an out pattern to have enough room to make the reception and turn up the field before going out of bounds.

Special Medium Routes

In addition to the three basic medium pass routes (in, out, and hook), there are three more pass routes that are run at the medium depth, but because of the time required to run the route, the quarterback has to take a five-step drop.

These three routes—cross, delay, and quick post (figure 5.7)—are all run with the timing of a medium pass route. Each requires special adjustments and comes into the inside of the field.

Cross. The cross, a variation of a short pattern, is the pattern that all good receivers run with success. When running the cross, the receiver sprints up the field for 4 yards and then angles to the inside, just as he would when running a slant route. He rolls over his inside foot and heads directly across the field at 8 yards. He makes sure he keeps running at full speed so the quarterback can accurately lead him with the ball. He turns his head around and focuses on the quarterback, preparing to catch the ball at any time.

As he comes across the field, he may find that his path angles slightly farther from the line of scrimmage. He should try to stay within 8 yards of the line of scrimmage and not allow himself to get so deep that he is running directly into coverage.

Delay. The delay pattern is run at the same 8-yard depth. At the start of this pattern, the receiver sprints off the line at a slight angle to the outside of the field and gives the defensive player the feeling that he is going deep. When he reaches 7 yards, the receiver stops his momentum upfield with his inside foot and spins back into the inside. As he spins, he momentarily turns his back on the defender. Once he comes out of the spin, he runs the remainder of the pass route just as he would on a cross.

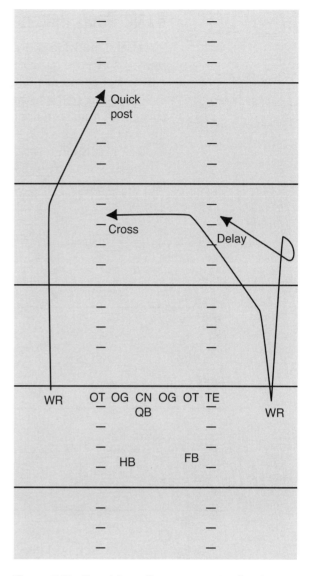

Figure 5.7 Special medium pass routes for the wide receiver: cross, delay, and quick post.

One major difference between the delay and the cross is that in the delay, the player expects the pass to come to him on his third or fourth step toward the center of the field. The angle release to the outside and the spin to the inside take additional time, which is why this pattern is run with medium pass timing.

Quick Post. The quick post is one pattern that requires no special move and is based solely on speed. The receiver comes straight off the line with as much speed as possible. At 8 yards, he breaks to the center of the field and continues up the field at a slight angle to the inside. The angle must keep him on the outside of the hash marks. The angle should be just enough to get some separation from the defensive back. The receiver must be alert for the ball at any time after running 5 yards from the breaking point.

Basic Deep Routes

Short and medium routes are the bread and butter for any wide receiver. Deep pass patterns are the icing on the cake. A wide receiver always feels a special thrill and a little boost in adrenaline when called on to run a deep pass pattern.

The timing of these patterns takes longer. To give the receiver time to run his deep route, the quarterback drops seven steps before delivering the ball. The offensive line has to block a few seconds longer on this type of pass. If the pass is complete, it often results in a touchdown.

The two basic deep patterns are the up and the post patterns (figure 5.8a). Both are run in the deep zone, 12 or more yards up the field from the line of scrimmage.

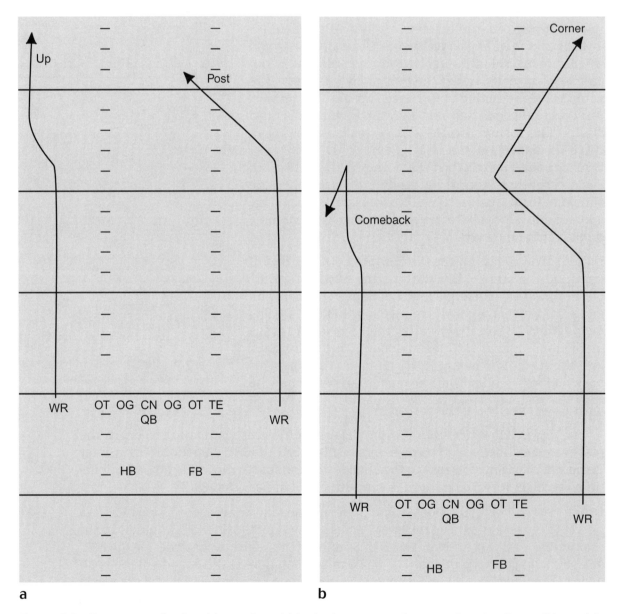

Figure 5.8 Deep routes for the wide receiver: *(a)* basic deep routes, the up and post patterns; *(b)* special deep routes, the comeback (off the up pattern) and the corner (off the post pattern).

To be successful, the receiver must run at full speed for the entire length of these pass patterns. The post and up routes are pass routes in which the receiver runs under the ball and often has to stretch to make the catch. He should always try to see his fingers and the ball at the same time as he attempts to make the reception.

Up Route.   Before releasing off the line of scrimmage, the receiver must observe where the defender is playing. If the defender is inside, the receiver wants to keep him there. If the defender is outside, the receiver wants to bring him away from the sideline as he comes off the line. The receiver uses a slight angle to the inside to position the defensive back where he wants him to be.

Ideally, on an up route the receiver has at least 5 yards between himself and the sideline so he has some room to adjust to the pass. When running the up pattern, the receiver must drive hard off the line of scrimmage and angle to position the defensive back where the receiver wants him. He must get to full speed and burst straight up the field, attacking the defender.

At 12 yards, he angles slightly to the outside to get clear of the defender. He sprints past the defensive back and heads straight up the field. He looks over his inside shoulder without breaking stride to pick up the flight of the ball as soon as possible, and he adjusts to the flight of the ball. He must be prepared to make the catch on his inside, directly in front, or, if the pass is perfectly thrown, over his outside shoulder away from the defender. There may be instances in which he will have to dive to make the catch.

The comeback (figure 5.8b) is a deep pass route that comes off the up pattern. It is difficult for a receiver to run the comeback pattern until he has success running the up route. Once the defensive back is worried that the receiver is going to run by him on the up pattern, the receiver is free to complete the comeback route.

At first, the comeback pattern is run exactly the same as an up route. The difference comes at 15 yards. To run the comeback properly, the receiver needs to get the defensive back turned and running up the field with him. At 15 yards, the receiver lowers his hips. At 17 yards, he plants his inside foot to stop his momentum and quickly turns to the sideline. He comes back toward the line of scrimmage at an angle and turns his head around to focus on the quarterback and the ball. He expects to make the catch at about 14 yards.

Once he makes the catch and secures the ball in his outside arm and hand, the safest thing for the receiver is to turn to the outside of the field and make as many yards as he can. If he turns back into the center of the field, he will run directly into defenders who are reacting to the pass.

Post Pattern.   The second deep pass pattern is the post route. The post is run into the center of the field away from the sideline.

The receiver looks to see where the defender is before the start of the play. If the defender is lined up and playing to the inside, the receiver angles slightly toward the sideline to get the defender to come with him as he sprints up the field, opening up the inside of the field. If the defender plays the receiver to the outside, the receiver should be able to sprint straight ahead for 12 yards before breaking to the inside. In short, the receiver wants to come off the line quickly, angle to position the defender if necessary, and burst straight at him to 12 yards. At 12 yards, he rolls over his inside foot and directs his path at 45 degrees to the center of the field.

The receiver must expect to run under the pass. This is not like the quick post, a medium pattern in which the quarterback tries to drill the ball. On the post pattern, the quarterback lofts the pass and it is the wide receiver's responsibility to keep running to make the catch. As soon as he makes his break and heads toward the center of the field, the receiver turns his head back to the quarterback and prepares to pick up the ball as it leaves the quarterback's hand. He may have to adjust his path slightly to make the catch. Often the receiver will need to reach out as he runs to catch the pass.

A wide receiver may have only one or two opportunities in a game to make a reception on a deep pass. It is important for the receiver to do everything possible to get open, concentrate on the ball, look it into his hands, and secure it before running for the score. When a defensive back is worried about the receiver going deep, it opens up the short and medium passing routes.

The wide receiver may use the corner route if the defensive back is playing way inside in order to stop the post pattern. The corner (figure 5.8b) is a deep route that comes off the post pattern. A receiver will have difficulty running the corner route until he has success running the basic post route. The corner route starts with the receiver selling the post pattern. The defensive back must be convinced that the receiver is going to run the post. It is essential for the receiver to turn the defender around and have the defender running as hard as he can to keep the receiver from going to the center of the field to make the catch. To help convince the defender, the receiver runs the first part of the corner pattern exactly the same as the post pattern.

The adjustment comes as the receiver starts toward the center of the field. After driving five or six hard steps toward the center of the field, the receiver leans his upper body to the outside and rolls over his outside foot. He breaks at a 45-degree angle to the corner of the field, keeping his speed and momentum as he breaks. He looks back over his outside shoulder to focus on the quarterback and pick up the flight of the ball.

On a corner pattern, the ball may hang in the air for a long time. The receiver may have to run 12 to 15 yards before he has a chance to make the catch. Ideally the ball comes to the receiver over his outside shoulder, away from any defensive backs. This allows the receiver to make the catch, secure the ball, and run up the sideline. Because it is a hard pass to throw, however, the receiver should watch for the ball to be anywhere. The pass may come directly over his head or to the inside. It is important for the receiver to see the flight of the pass as soon as possible, because seeing the ball early in its flight allows the receiver to turn his head to the correct side and position his hands so he can see both the ball and his hands as he makes the catch.

Short Pass Routes

Purpose: To give the wide receiver experience running short pass routes.

Procedure:
1. The coach lines up 10 yards in front of the wide receiver.
2. The coach calls out the short pass route and the wide receiver gets into position for the play.
3. The coach begins the play and the wide receiver runs the pass route.
4. The coach offers feedback on the wide receiver's performance.

Variations: This drill is also good for practicing medium and deep pass routes. For medium routes, the coach lines up 20 yards in front of the wide receiver. For deep routes, the coach lines up 10 yards away and faces the wide receiver. He can vary his position from inside to outside.

Coaching Points: When learning any pass route, the receiver should make sure he has a good stance, takes a forward step, and threatens going deep on each route. He should break his route at the proper depth, use good technique when changing direction, and turn his head back to the quarterback at the earliest possible moment.

Out and In Patterns

Purpose: To give the wide receiver experience running out and in pass routes.

Procedure:

1. One wide receiver lines up as a defensive back inside or outside of the other wide receiver, 8 yards off the line.
2. The play starts on the coach's command and the wide receiver runs the route.
3. The other wide receiver drops back as if he were a defender reacting to the wide receiver's movements.
4. The coach offers feedback on the wide receiver's performance.

Coaching Points: Check that the receiver is angling his run to position the defender. On his break, make certain that he is keeping his speed and momentum.

Special Medium Routes

Purpose: To give the wide receiver experience running cross, delay, and quick post pass routes.

Procedure:

1. The coach stands 20 yards away and faces the wide receiver. A defensive back sets up to cover the wide receiver.
2. On the coach's command, the wide receiver runs the called route. The coach observes his moves.
3. The defensive back should drop straight back as the wide receiver runs each route.

Coaching Points: Make certain that the receiver comes off of the line at the proper angle to run each route. It is important for the receiver to get up to speed as soon as possible after making his break and to look for the ball as soon as possible.

Corner and Comeback

Purpose: To give the wide receiver experience running the corner and comeback routes.

Procedure:

1. The coach lines up 20 yards away and faces the wide receiver.
2. On the coach's command, the wide receiver runs the specified route.
3. The coach observes the wide receiver's movements and provides feedback.

Coaching Points: The receiver must sell the deep patterns that these two patterns build on. He must run the base pattern hard before making the break on either of these patterns.

BLOCKING

Any offensive football team with a strong running game has wide receivers who have the desire and know-how to block. When a running play results in a touchdown, it means the wide receiver on the side of the play executed a good block on one of the defensive backs. Wide receiver blocking for running plays is 60 percent desire and 40 percent technique. When a receiver has the desire to block, he can easily learn the proper techniques.

For a wide receiver, blocking downfield is a lot like tackling for a defensive player. It requires desire. To block effectively, a wide receiver must have a burning desire to get the job accomplished and the pride to constantly try to succeed. Size is not the issue. There are a number of small wide receivers today who block effectively on every running play. When the goal is to become a complete wide receiver, blocking must be worked on with complete focus.

A wide receiver who is blocking wants to position himself between the defender and the ball carrier. The receiver must think in terms of maneuvering his body into this position. The goal is to force the defensive player to come through the receiver to reach the running back and make the tackle.

If the receiver's blocking assignment is the defender lined up directly in front of him, the receiver must drive off the line and create indecision in the defender's mind. If the defender keeps backing up or covering a deep zone, then the receiver should continue his drive and use the glide part of his release from 5 to 12 yards to position himself.

The instant the defender stops his backpedal and focuses on the ball carrier, the receiver must shorten his stride and bring his body under control. The closer he comes to the defender, the more he widens his base. He keeps his feet moving in short, choppy steps as he positions himself between the defender and the ball carrier. As the defender comes closer, the receiver focuses on the middle of the numbers on the defender's jersey. In preparation for the block, the receiver bends at his knees but not his waist, keeping his back straight and his head up (figure 5.9a).

At the point of contact, the receiver keeps his elbows close to the sides of his body (figure 5.9b). His forearms are up and angled into the center of his chest. Both hands are open with the fingers up, palms facing the defender. The receiver hits the defender in the chest with the heels of both hands with as much force as he can generate. He generates power for the block first with the big muscles in the legs and then with the up and out motion of the hands and arms.

After making the initial contact, the receiver needs to keep his balance, gather himself, and hit the defender again and again until the whistle blows. If the defender

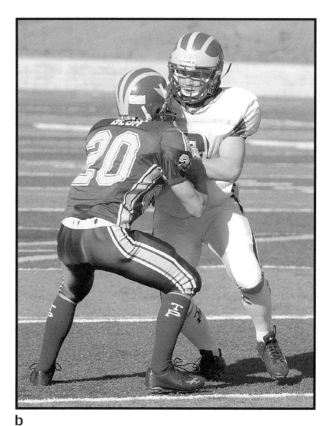

a   b

Figure 5.9 Wide receiver blocking: *(a)* receiver bends his knees; *(b)* receiver makes contact.

fails to make the tackle, the receiver has done an outstanding job even if he never knocks the defender down.

When blocking downfield, the receiver must anticipate that the defender will try to avoid the block and go to one side or the other. The receiver will be able to react easily to any attempt by the defensive player to go around him to the ball carrier if the receiver shortens his stride and widens his base.

Reacting to the Defender

Purpose: To give the wide receiver practice blocking a defender.

Procedure

1. The coach or another wide receiver lines up 8 yards from the wide receiver, holding a dummy.
2. When the wide receiver releases, the coach or other wide receiver backs up 6 yards and then steps up, allowing the wide receiver to block.
3. The wide receiver blocks on the dummy.

Coaching Points: Begin the drill at half speed, then speed it up as the wide receiver becomes proficient in blocking. Ultimately run the drill at full speed. The receiver should know where the ball is going to be run so that he can position himself to the right or left of the defender.

6

Tight End

Playing tight end involves a combination of the necessary skills to play offensive lineman, wide receiver, and running back. No other position on the team requires such a mix of abilities. On one play a tight end may make the key block to spring the running back, and on the next play he may jump high in the air to make a catch. This chapter focuses on the skills needed to be a top tight end, including stance, blocking, and pass routes.

STANCE

The tight end has to block like an offensive lineman, but at the same time he has to release off the line and run pass routes like a wide receiver. He must have a balanced stance that allows him to accomplish both tasks.

The tight end uses the basic three-point stance (figure 6.1). To get into the three-point stance, the tight end stands with his feet even and shoulder-width apart. His toes point straight ahead. He lowers his body by bending his knees, keeping his back straight. He rests both forearms on his inner thighs and reaches out with one hand. He then takes a small step back with the foot on the same side as the down hand.

The down hand extends straight out and down and contacts the ground just in front of the tight end's shoulders. The toes of the back foot are even with the middle of the front foot. His weight is evenly distributed on both feet, especially if the first step changes with each play.

Once he has put his hand down and adjusted his back foot, the tight end needs to focus on keeping his back straight, his shoulders even, and his head up. He must be sure he does not lean to one side or the other. Leaning or looking anywhere but straight ahead gives the defense a good idea where the tight end is going and whom he will block.

Figure 6.1 Three-point stance.

BLOCKING

The real challenge to playing tight end is learning to be an effective blocker. A tight end must understand that during a running play he becomes an additional offensive lineman. On every wide running play to his side, the tight end's block is at the point of attack. To be a good blocker, the tight end must have good technique, understand how defenders will play against him, and possess the desire to successfully complete the block.

Tight ends can learn all blocks by using a blocking bag or blocking sled, but they must remember that the real defender will be in motion, not stationary. This chapter focuses on the tight end's blocking role in each of the blocks. The techniques and drills for each of the blocks a tight end may use during the game on running plays—drive, hook, angle, running drive, double team, and combination—are covered in chapter 3, beginning on page 41. Please refer to that chapter for information on technique.

The tight end uses the drive block against a defensive lineman or a linebacker who is playing directly in front of the tight end. The goal of the drive block is to move the defender back off the line of scrimmage. A good drive block starts with getting out of the stance instantly on the snap. It is essential to focus on the defender because he may stunt to one side or the other. When he makes contact, the tight end drives forward with both arms and hands. To get maximum leverage and force, he keeps his elbows close to his ribs. The palms of both hands contact the middle of the defender's body in a strong, forceful manner.

Although he makes contact with his hands, his legs do the majority of the work. The instant he makes contact, he pushes his hips forward and up, gathering his legs under him while driving his feet with short, choppy steps. For most tight ends, this last step is the most difficult. The tendency is to stop moving the feet at the moment of contact. Once the forward thrust stops, it is very difficult to get started again, and the tight end usually ends up just leaning against the defender. The tight end should pick a spot two to three feet past the defender and keep driving until he reaches that spot. This enables the tight end to finish the block successfully.

The tight end uses the hook block against a defensive player who lines up in front of him. The hook is a difficult block. Trying to hook a linebacker or defensive lineman lined up on the tight end's outside shoulder is the hardest of all. The primary objective of the hook block is to prevent the defender from coming across the line of scrimmage and stop his pursuit. Once he is in this position and has stopped the defender's movement across the line, the tight end needs to continue driving with his feet, using short, powerful steps as he would in a drive block.

On an angle block, the tight end blocks a defender who lines up opposite the offensive player to the tight end's right or left. The defensive lineman is focused on another offensive player when the play begins, so his reaction to the tight end and his block is secondary. Blocking the defender before he is able to react is the reason the tight end must execute the angle block with as much speed and quickness as possible. Another reason for quickness is that the tight end must stop the defender's penetration. The defender will be charging straight ahead, so the tight end must anticipate the block. The tight end should practice the angle block to both his right and left until he can execute it correctly in either direction.

With the variations in defensive alignment, the tight end may block a linebacker who is not on the line of scrimmage. To get this done, the tight end must be familiar with the running drive block, which blocks a linebacker playing off the line of scrimmage directly in front of the tight end or to his inside. Moving in the right path is essential when blocking someone who is not on the line of scrimmage. The tight end's quick start is crucial to his success when blocking a linebacker on the run. The tight end must keep a wide base and stay low as he comes off the line. If the linebacker is inside of the tight end or in front of the tackle, the tight end must be sure he takes his first step with his inside foot. He must always anticipate the linebacker charging straight ahead on a blitz. The tight end's goal is to drive the linebacker off the line of scrimmage back toward his own goal line.

For the double team block, the tight end works with another offensive player to block one defensive player (figure 6.2). This block requires practice to perfect, but the results are well worth the effort. Both players must work in unison and toward the same goal as they learn this block. The double team is not just one block, but a combination of two blocks. When executing the block, the offensive player directly in front of the defender uses a drive block. The offensive player who blocks from the side of the defender uses a modified angle block. Combining these two blocks results in a double team block. Based on the type of offense the team runs, a tight end may be part of a double team block with either an offensive tackle or with an offensive player who lines up in the wing position outside of the tight end. When working with the tackle, the tight end is the angle blocker. When working with the wing, the tight end is the drive blocker.

In combination blocking, the tight end and offensive tackle are responsible for blocking two defensive players (figure 6.3). The two players to be blocked are usually a defensive lineman who is lined up on the offensive tackle and a linebacker who is lined up off the line. Players use a combination block against stunting or slanting defenses, defenses in which the defensive linemen move quickly into a gap on the snap of the ball. The combination block starts with an attack on the defensive player on the line of scrimmage. The defensive end is lined up on the line of

Figure 6.2 Tight end helping with a double team block.

Figure 6.3 TE and OT executing a combination block on a defensive lineman and a linebacker.

scrimmage directly in front of the tackle, while the outside linebacker is in front of the tight end. The play is run to the opposite side of the formation. The goal is to keep both defensive linemen from pursuing down the line of scrimmage. Players may also use a combination block on an outside wide running play versus a defense in which the defensive lineman is in front of the tight end and the linebacker is in front of the offensive tackle. The roles of the tight end and the offensive tackle are reversed. Both players take their first steps with their outside feet.

PASS PLAYS

In a pass play, the tight end must have a good release off the line of scrimmage. He must quickly move from his starting position into the defensive secondary. Most tight ends use a three-point stance, although some may use an upright two-point stance, especially when flexing away from the offensive tackle. No matter the stance, the ability to quickly get off the line is vital to the passing game.

The tight end's release is more difficult when a defender lines up directly in front of him, which usually happens. The tight end's defender may be a linebacker, a defensive lineman, or, in some situations, a defensive back. The first step is crucial when releasing off the line. With a defender in front of him, the tight end needs to take an angle step with his back foot to the side of his release (figure 6.4a). This must be a forward step, one that starts the tight end moving up the field. If the right foot is back and he releases to the right of the defender, the tight end should step slightly to the right as he brings the back foot up. When releasing to the left from the same stance, the tight end needs to bring the back foot up and slightly across his body to create a path to the left of the defender.

This first step creates a small separation from the defender, giving the tight end the time to bring the arm closest to the defender forward and swing it hard up and in front of his own shoulder (figure 6.4b). This ripping-up motion, if done with force

a

b

Figure 6.4 Tight end releases off the line: *(a)* first angle step; *(b)* tight end swings arm to keep defender's hands off his jersey.

and determination, is usually enough to get the defender's hands off the tight end's jersey.

The tight end must stay low and come off the ball hard. Spending time trying to fake the defender at the line of scrimmage only slows the release and keeps the tight end from getting into his pass pattern.

Short and Medium Pass Routes

Once the tight end has learned the stance, start, and release, he is ready to learn to run short and medium pass routes.

For short routes (5 yards or less), the tight end goes directly from his release into his route. Timing is crucial on short routes. For short routes such as a look-in or short-out pattern (figure 6.5), the tight end does not have time to move the defensive back to where the tight end would like him to be when he makes his final cut. On all short routes, the quarterback takes a short three-step drop and delivers the ball. The offensive line blocks aggressively for only a short time, so every short pass must be thrown quickly to be successful.

Distance and momentum are important in short routes. As he releases up the field on a short route, the tight end needs to know the distance he should run before he breaks. If he is going to the outside at 5 yards, a short-out pattern, he rolls over the foot in the direction he is going. He does not plant and step as this will only stop his momentum. If coming to the inside on a look-in pass, again the tight end must know the distance he needs to go and then redirect his body to the inside. In both of these short patterns, the tight end bursts into his final move and brings his head around quickly. He establishes good vision of the quarterback and gets his hands into position to catch the ball. The tight end has to stay alert. The ball comes to him very quickly and he probably will be hit the instant he makes the catch, so he must make certain the ball is secure.

For medium routes, which are 10 to 15 yards, the tight end adds two more elements to his pattern. As he releases up the field, he determines how the defensive back is playing him. Is the defender on his inside or outside? The tight end can influence the position of the defensive back and get open by angling his route slightly away from the direction he wishes to go in his final cut.

When running an in pattern after coming straight up the field for 3 yards, the tight end angles to the outside for 5 yards (figure 6.6). This slight adjustment in his route

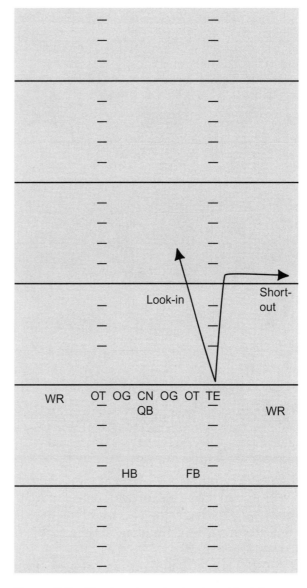

Figure 6.5 Short routes: short-out and look-in pass.

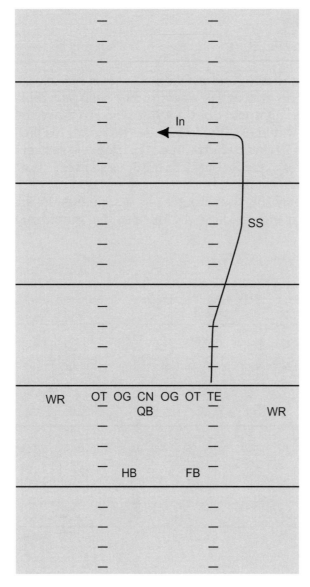

Figure 6.6 TE running an in pattern against a SS to the outside.

makes the defender leave the area where the tight end wants to go. If the defender is inside the tight end, the defender will come with the tight end. If the defender is outside, he will go even wider, trying to stay outside the tight end. Once the tight end sees that the defender is moving with him, he again directs his pattern straight up the field. This move should convince the defender that the tight end is going deep. Ideally the defender will turn and start running toward his own goal line.

After sprinting up the field for 5 more yards, the tight end is ready to make his final cut. He keeps his speed and momentum by leaning his upper body to the inside and rolling over his inside foot. The tight end may feel as if he is rounding off the turn, but the important thing is that he maintains speed.

Once he's in the burst of the final turn, the tight end needs to turn his head and focus on the quarterback. The quarterback may be under pressure and not see the tight end the instant he makes his cut, so it is vital for the tight end to continue his burst and keep moving across the field until the ball is thrown.

When running an out pattern, the tight end first angles to the inside and then sprints up the field before making his cut to the outside. The tight end should practice running all four paths until he feels comfortable with them. Only by getting open will he ever have the opportunity to make a catch.

When running the hook route, the tight end must drive straight up the field and not worry about positioning the defender. His goal is to make the defender think that he is running deep. When he reaches 10 yards, he shortens his stride, lowers his hips, and stops his forward momentum by planting his outside foot. He quickly turns back to the inside and faces the quarterback, bringing both hands up to the center of his chest. He immediately looks for the ball and moves toward the ball to make the catch.

A cross route is not run as deep as the other medium routes, but it requires the same timing. When running a cross route, the tight end should take an inside release off the line of scrimmage if possible and drive up the field, similar to a look-in route (figure 6.5, page 107). The tight end rolls over his inside foot at 6 yards and starts running across the field at full speed. He increases his depth slightly as he runs across the field, though he never goes deeper than 10 yards. He turns his head and focuses on the quarterback. He expects the pass any time after he passes the offensive center. The tight end often runs this route when the play requires the quarterback to move out of the pocket to throw the ball.

Deep Pass Routes

Deep patterns take longer to develop, therefore the timing of these patterns takes longer. To allow time to run the deep route, the quarterback drops seven steps before delivering the ball. The offensive line has to block a few seconds longer for a deep pass. When successful, this pass often results in a touchdown.

There are three basic deep pass routes— seam, post, and corner—and all three require speed. All are run in the deep zone, 12 or more yards up the field away from the line of scrimmage. To have success with these three patterns, the tight end needs to run at full speed for the entire length of the pass pattern. For the post, corner, and seam pass routes, the tight end runs under the ball and often has to stretch to make the catch. The tight end should try to see his fingers and the ball at the same time when attempting to make the reception.

The first deep pattern is the seam pattern. Before the start of the play, the tight end should determine the alignment of the safety on his side of the field. Trying to position the defender is OK, but the tight end must never sacrifice speed to move a defender. When running the seam pattern the tight end tries to release outside of any defensive man in front of him. He immediately gets his speed and momentum going straight up the field. At 12 yards, he bends to the outside while still going up the field. He gets into a position that allows him to run up the field 5 to 7 yards outside of the hash marks. At about 15 yards, he comes slightly back to the inside and establishes a sight path to the quarterback and the ball. He picks up (locates) the ball as soon as it leaves the quarterback's hand by looking over his inside shoulder. He does not break stride. He may need to adjust to the flight of the ball, and he should expect to make the catch on his inside, directly in front, or over his outside shoulder (figure 6.7). Speed is crucial the entire time. Regardless of where the defender is, the tight end cannot slow down. He needs to keep his momentum going up the field at all cost. There may be times when he has to dive to catch the ball.

The second deep pass pattern is the post route. The post pattern is run into the center of the field away from the sideline. The tight end looks to see where the defender is before the start of the play. If the defender is lined up and playing the tight end on the inside, the tight end angles slightly toward the sideline to entice the defender to come with him, opening up the inside of the field. If the defender is playing the tight end on the outside, the tight end probably will be able to sprint straight ahead for 12 yards before making his break to the inside. When running the post, the tight end releases to the outside, comes off the line quickly, angles to position

Figure 6.7 Tight end makes the catch over his outside shoulder.

Figure 6.8 Tight end makes the catch in front by reaching out.

the defender if necessary, and bursts straight at him to 12 yards. At 12 yards, the tight end rolls over his inside foot and directs his path at 45 degrees into the center of the field. He expects to run under the pass. On this pattern, the pass will be thrown with loft and it is the tight end's responsibility to keep running to make the catch. As soon as he makes his break and heads toward the center of the field, the tight end turns his head back to the quarterback, ready to pick up the ball as it leaves the quarterback's hand. He may have to adjust his path slightly to make the catch. Often he will make the catch in front by reaching out as he runs (figure 6.8).

The third pattern, the corner route, is run off the post pattern. To run the corner route successfully, the tight end must sell the post pattern to the defender. The tight end runs up the field exactly the same way as in the post and cuts to the inside. After running 3 or 4 yards toward the center of the field, bringing the defensive back with him, the tight end makes a second cut. This cut is on a 45-degree angle back to the corner of the field. He keeps his momentum by rolling over his outside foot as he goes to the corner of the field. In this pass pattern, the ball is in the air for a long time. The tight end must run hard and expect to travel at least 15 to 20 yards before making the catch. He looks back over his outside shoulder to pick up the quarterback and the ball. He may need to make adjustments to his route as he heads for the ball.

A tight end is going to have only one or two opportunities, at most, to actually make a reception on a deep pass in a game. It is important to do everything possible to get open, concentrate on the ball, look it into his hands, and secure the ball before running for the score. There is no better feeling for any receiver than running deep, seeing the ball spiraling his way, making the catch, and running into the end zone.

Solo Practice

Purpose: To give the tight end experience in running basic pass routes by himself.

Procedure: The tight end can practice all of the basic patterns alone by following this procedure:

1. Decide which pattern to run.
2. Get into a good stance.
3. Execute a proper release.
4. Picture where the defensive man is going to be.
5. Run the route quickly.
6. Face the quarterback at the right time in the pattern.
7. Visualize the ball's path.
8. Go through the motions of making the catch and securing the ball.

Coaching Points: Check that the tight end is making his break at the proper depth for each pass route. He should keep his momentum during the entire route. Check that he turns his head back to the quarterback as soon as he can.

Running Short Routes

Purpose: To give the tight end experience running short routes.

Procedure

1. The coach lines up 10 yards downfield. A tight end and a linebacker line up as if on the line of scrimmage. A tight end can take the place of the linebacker if a linebacker isn't available.
2. The coach calls a short route and signals the start of the play.
3. On the coach's signal, the tight end releases around the linebacker and runs the short route.
4. The coach observes the tight end's release and pattern and offers feedback.

Variation: The same setup is helpful for practicing medium routes, including the in, out, and hook routes. The coach should line up 20 yards downfield.

Coaching Points: In all of these drills, make certain that the tight end is stepping forward with his first step, that he is releasing on the correct side of the defensive man, and that he is moving at full speed as soon as possible. On medium pass routes the tight end should adjust his route to position the defender away from his final cut.

Running Deep Routes

Purpose: To give the tight end experience running deep routes.

Procedure

1. For the seam route, the coach lines up 10 yards downfield and outside the tight end. A tight end and a linebacker line up on the line of scrimmage. A tight end can take the place of the linebacker if a linebacker isn't available.
2. The coach calls the seam route and signals the start of the play.
3. On the coach's signal, the tight end releases around the linebacker and runs the seam route.
4. The coach observes the tight end's release and pattern and offers feedback.

Variation: The same setup is good for practicing other deep routes as well. For the post or corner patterns, a defensive back or another tight end line up 8 yards down the field inside or outside the tight end's original position.

Coaching Points: Check the tight end's release and drive up the field. He should break on both patterns at the correct depth. On the corner route the tight end must sell the post before breaking to the outside.

7

Defensive Lineman

Defensive linemen make contact on every play, guaranteed. They are in the middle of the action, colliding with the offensive player who is trying to block them. Unlike their teammates, who may be lined up off the line of scrimmage, defensive linemen instantly experience action. Defensive linemen need to stay focused to see and understand what is taking place.

The challenge for the defensive lineman is to try to defeat the offensive blocker on every play and then attack the ball carrier. Learning to play this physically demanding position can be frustrating, especially when first starting out. A defensive lineman doesn't know who is blocking him or who has the ball. It will become easier for him to see more of what is happening as he gains experience.

To become a good defensive lineman, a player must learn the following techniques: using the proper stance, moving on the ball, defeating and separating from blocks, and rushing the passer. Each of these techniques help players become better defensive linemen, helping to ensure success while playing the defensive line.

STANCE

The defensive lineman's stance depends on the type of block he faces and any adjustments he needs to make based on down and distance. The closer the defensive lineman is to the ball before the play begins, the greater the number of players who will be there to block him. As the player moves to the outside, he may see several blockers, but he usually has a little time to see what is happening. His beginning stance must allow him to react to the wide variety of blocks he faces.

The stance depends on the style of defense the team is using. Beginning players may use a four-point stance, while more experienced players may use a three-point stance. Defensive linemen who face running teams should use a balanced stance, while defensive linemen on a team that faces a passing team may need more of a staggered stance.

To get into a three- or four-point stance, the player begins by standing with his feet even and about shoulder-width apart. The coach should check to see that the defensive lineman's toes point straight ahead. While keeping his head up and back straight, the defensive lineman starts bending his knees until he can rest his forearms on the inside of either thigh. From this position, the player can reach forward and down with both hands and arms for the four-point stance (figure 7.1a). He places his hands on the ground slightly in front of his shoulders. In this position, the player's weight is distributed evenly over both hands and both feet. To get into a three-point stance, all he has to do is lift one hand off the ground, rest the elbow on the knee, and extend the forearm forward and up. The palm of the hand no longer on the ground should be open with the fingers spread and pointing up (figure 7.1b).

On a passing down or if the defensive lineman is playing on or outside the offensive tackle, he should slightly stagger his feet. He steps back with his inside foot so that the toe is slightly behind the heel of his other foot. In a three-point stance, the hand on the ground and the back foot are on the same side of the player's body. The heel of his back foot should be off the ground. See the section on rushing the passer for more about the staggered stance (page 125).

In a good stance, the defensive lineman's head is up and his eyes look straight ahead. He needs to keep his shoulders even and his back straight. He should feel ready to react to a block from the right, left, or from straight ahead.

a   b

Figure 7.1 Stances: *(a)* four-point stance; *(b)* three-point stance.

MOVING ON THE BALL

While offensive players have the snap count to tell them when the play begins, the ball and any movement on the offensive line serve as the sign for defensive linemen to move. Because of the nearness of the offensive blockers, if the defensive lineman hesitates, the offensive blockers will probably defeat him. A successful defensive lineman has the ability to quickly get off the ball and into position to defeat offensive blockers.

Regardless of the stance, the defensive lineman must condition himself to concentrate on moving the instant an offensive lineman or the ball moves. On his first step, he must stay low and not rise to look for the ball carrier. A defensive lineman has to charge straight ahead, take a control step to his right or left, or take a crossover step to his right or left. With each of these movements, his first step must be quick.

If playing a control technique—one in which there is no penetration across the line of scrimmage—the defensive lineman's first step is a quick lateral step. The foot he steps with depends on the defense called and the gap that is his responsibility. He always takes the control step with the foot on the same side as the direction of his movement. The defensive lineman should practice stepping in both directions.

For a penetrating start with fast movement into a gap between two offensive players, the defensive lineman may need to use a crossover start. Instead of stepping laterally with the near foot as he did in a control start, he takes his first step across his body with the opposite foot. If he is moving to his right, his first step is with his left foot. If he is attacking the gap to his left, his first step is across his body with his right foot. The crossover start may bring his shoulders up more than when he charges straight ahead or uses a control step, but on all three starts the defensive lineman wants to stay as low as possible with his shoulders square to the line of scrimmage.

DEFEATING BLOCKS

Because the offensive man in front of the defensive lineman is in position to be the first to block him, the defensive lineman must concentrate on this offensive lineman and look for the drive or hook block (figure 7.2). The next offensive player in position to block the defensive lineman is the offensive player to his immediate right or left. After these two players, the near back, if there is one, or the offside guard may be secondary blockers.

When beginning to play defensive line, the defensive lineman must think in terms of a blocking progression. He should ask himself which offensive player can block him, when the offensive player can block him, and what type of block the offensive player will use. Once he knows the answers to these questions, he is on his way to becoming a top-flight defensive lineman.

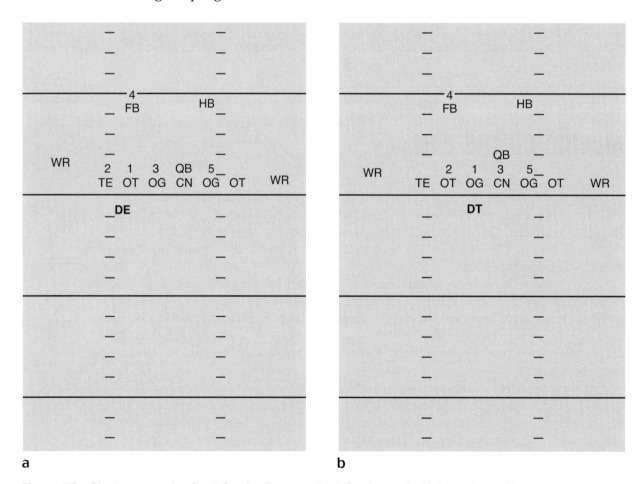

a   b

Figure 7.2 Block progression for defensive linemen: *(a)* defensive end; *(b)* defensive tackle.

Drive Block

One of the first offensive blocks a defensive lineman must learn to expect, recognize, and defeat is the drive block. In this block, the offensive lineman directly in front of the defensive lineman tries to drive the defensive lineman off the line of scrimmage.

As the blocker moves toward the defensive lineman, it is crucial that the defensive lineman start his momentum toward the offensive blocker (figure 7.3a). To meet and defeat the blocker's power, the defensive lineman must have a wide base and take only short power steps.

At contact, the defensive lineman keeps his shoulder pads even with or slightly below the blocker's shoulder pads (figure 7.3b). With his shoulder pads in this position, the defensive lineman will be able to keep the blocker from getting underneath him and driving him off the line of scrimmage.

As he steps forward and his shoulder pads make contact with the offensive blocker, the defensive lineman slides his helmet to the side of his gap responsibility. The defensive lineman should always make contact with the blocker with his pads, not his helmet. The defensive lineman is responsible for one side of the drive blocker or the other unless he is responsible for the running lanes on both sides of the blocker (two-gap responsibility).

The instant the defensive lineman makes contact with his shoulder pads, he extends his arms so that the palms of both hands make contact at the numbers of the offensive blocker's jersey (figure 7.3c). From this point he can straighten his arms, get separation from the blocker, and be in position to throw the blocker aside and move to attack the ball carrier.

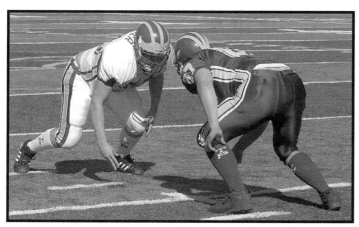

Figure 7.3 Defeating a drive block: *(a)* the DL gains momentum as he moves toward the blocker; *(b)* at contact the DL's shoulder pads are even with or slightly below the blocker's pads; *(c)* he uses his arms to get separation from the blocker.

a

b

c

If he takes a lateral or crossover step to secure a gap, the defensive lineman moves directly to one side of the blocker or the other on the snap of the ball. In this style of defense, it is important for the defensive lineman to fight back into the blocker and not let the blocker use the defensive lineman's own momentum to drive him out of the hole.

Hook Block

Like the drive block, the hook block is used by an offensive blocker who lines up directly in front of the defensive lineman. The goal of the drive block is to keep the defensive lineman from penetrating across the line of scrimmage and to move him back toward his own goal line. The objective of the hook block is different. Now the offensive player wants to stop the defensive lineman's penetration and force him to move to either his right or left.

When the play begins, the defensive lineman needs to see immediately that the blocker is moving laterally to his right or left and not coming directly at him. The blocker will try to get his helmet outside the defensive lineman's shoulder pad so he can drive the shoulder away from his movement into the defensive lineman's belly and hip.

As the defensive lineman takes his first short step forward, he sees the blocker's helmet and shoulder pads moving to the right or left. The defensive lineman quickly extends both his arms into the blocker. He tries to make contact with the palms of both hands on the blocker's shoulder pads (figure 7.4). If he can get his hands and arms extended quickly enough into the blocker, he will have greater power at the moment of contact. The blocker's momentum may still be lateral, not forward. As his hands make contact, the defensive lineman continues to take short power steps and drive the blocker back across the line of scrimmage into the offensive backfield.

In this position, the defensive lineman is able to keep the blocker from using his legs or shoulder pads to get into the defensive lineman's body. The defensive lineman should keep his head up. Once he locates the ball carrier, he sheds the blocker and tries to get in on the tackle.

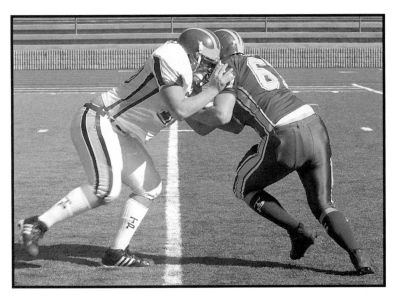

Figure 7.4 Defeating a hook block.

Angle Block

One of the most difficult blocks a defensive lineman faces is the angle block. The difficulty comes from the closeness of the blocker and the fact that the blocker is not lined up directly in front of the defensive lineman. The defensive lineman must focus on the offensive lineman directly in front, and at the same time, the defensive lineman must see in his side vision the offensive lineman to his right and to his left, men in position to attack him. The challenge in defeating the angle block is that the defensive lineman must start forward first toward the player in front of him, then quickly redirect his momentum to the right or left.

When defeating an angle block, the defensive lineman's goals are to redirect his momentum into the blocker, stop the blocker's momentum, and prevent the blocker from driving him off the line of scrimmage. If the defensive lineman is ever in a situation in which he feels he is losing this battle, he should drop down to his hands and knees, trying to create as big a pile as possible.

The offensive blocker using an angle block comes at the defensive lineman from the side. It is impossible for the defensive lineman to turn and meet this block squarely as he did when playing the drive or hook block. The second he sees that the offensive player in front is not going to block him, the defensive lineman must see if the offensive player on his right or left is coming at him. The instant he determines this, he needs to take a short step at the blocker with the foot on the same side as the block (figure 7.5a).

The defensive lineman will be able to make contact with the offensive man with his near shoulder pad only (figure 7.5b). Keeping his knees bent, he redirects as much of his momentum into the blocker as possible. As his shoulder pad makes contact, the defensive lineman tries to lift his forearm on the side of the block into the chest of the offensive blocker (figure 7.5c).

As he makes contact, he continues to drive his legs using short, choppy power steps as he works to defeat the blocker. Keeping his leg drive and staying low are two important techniques when reacting to this block. After he has stepped into the blocker, made contact with his shoulder pad, and struck a blow with his forearm, he can try to turn his entire body into the blocker. As his far shoulder comes around, he tries to strike the blocker's shoulder pad with the palm of his far arm. He may be able to get under the shoulder pad and knock the blocker off balance.

Scoop or Combination Block

Now that the defensive lineman knows how to defeat one offensive blocker who is attacking him, he can focus on defeating blocks in which two offensive players attack him.

The first block of this type is the scoop or combination block. In the scoop block, the offensive player directly in front of the defensive lineman fires out at the defensive lineman in a way that makes him think that the blocker is trying to hook block him. The defensive lineman's natural reaction is to defeat the hook block. All his attention is directed at the offensive player in front of him, and his first instinct is to put both of his hands on the first blocker.

As the defensive lineman makes contact, he will feel that the blocker is not really trying to hook him, but instead is trying to stop his pursuit. The offensive blocker's job is to momentarily stop the defensive lineman's penetration and lateral movement. The blocker is setting up the defensive lineman for the final block by the offensive lineman opposite the first blocker's movement.

Once the first blocker has stopped the defensive lineman, he pushes off the defensive lineman, releases on the side of the fake hook block, and continues up the field to get in position to block a linebacker. After the initial blocker releases, the second blocker tries to position himself directly in front of the defensive lineman. Then he tries to work his way around the defensive lineman, just as in a hook block. The second blocker's job is not to drive the defensive lineman off the line of scrimmage, but to position himself so that the defensive lineman cannot pursue down the line to tackle the ball carrier. The second blocker steps laterally down the line, fighting to get a head-up position on the defensive lineman. The second blocker is most vulnerable when he is moving down the line and not attacking the defensive lineman directly.

a

b

c

Figure 7.5 Defeating an angle block: *(a)* DL steps to the blocker; *(b)* DL makes contact with his near shoulder pad; *(c)* DL uses his forearm to push the blocker back.

The defensive lineman must quickly recognize this block as the play begins. He should notice that the offensive player in front of him is not as low as he would be on a normal hook block. Instead of seeing his shoulder pads, the defensive lineman sees the numbers on the offensive blocker's jersey. This should alert the defensive lineman that the blocker is faking a hook block and the defensive lineman must be prepared for an attack by another offensive blocker.

As soon as the defensive lineman senses that the offensive player in front of him is not a true blocker but is only setting him up, he must charge straight up the field and try to engage the second blocker (figure 7.6). The second blocker will not come at the defensive lineman with much power in the beginning, so the defensive lineman should try to get both hands into the blocker's chest as quickly as possible. He must keep a good defensive position with his head up, back straight, and knees bent, using the large muscles of the legs to push the blocker back to the offensive side of the ball.

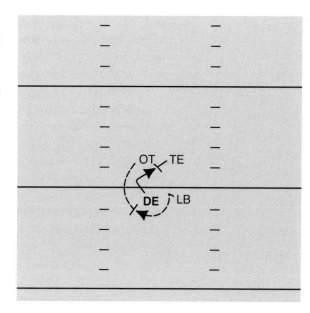

Figure 7.6 Defeating a combination block by engaging the second blocker.

From this position, the defensive lineman works his head and body to the side of the first blocker's release and fights down the line. The defensive lineman must never let the scoop blocker cut off his lateral movement. He should get into the pursuit path that will take him to the ball carrier.

Double Team Block

There is no greater challenge for a defensive lineman than fighting off a double team block. For most of the game only one offensive player blocks the defensive lineman. During a scoop block, two offensive linemen block him but not at the same time. On a double team block, all that changes. Two offensive players block the defensive lineman for the entire play, so he has to defeat the combined power and weight of two blockers instead of one.

A double team block is an offensive block executed in unison by the offensive player directly in front of the defensive lineman and an adjacent offensive blocker to the right or left. For a defensive end playing in front of an offensive tackle, the double team block usually comes from the offensive tackle and the tight end just to the outside. If the defensive lineman lines up in front of one of the offensive guards, the double team block will come from the offensive guard and the offensive tackle or the center. When the defensive lineman is in the middle of the action and lines up in front of the center, he can expect the center and either guard to be involved in the double team.

The double team block is not one block but a combination of two blocks. The offensive blocker in front of the defensive lineman executes the drive block, and the offensive player coming at the defensive lineman from the side executes the angle block. Combining the angle and drive blocks results in a double team block. The objective of these two offensive players who are working together is to drive the defensive lineman off and down the line of scrimmage. They want to stand him up and then, shoulder to shoulder, drive him out of the hole.

The defensive lineman first reacts to the offensive blocker in front of him, so he will be working to stop the drive block. To do this, the defensive lineman has both hands on the drive blocker and concentrates on defeating the drive block (figure 7.7a). The instant he sees that he is the target of a double team block, the defensive lineman must prepare for the angle block that is coming from the side. He lowers his body and directs as much weight as he can into the angle blocker (figure 7.7b).

Seldom will the defensive lineman have the strength or power to defeat both blockers. If he can just create a pile at the site of the block, he will have effectively defeated the double team block and won the battle. Staying as low as the blockers or lower is very important if he is to win the battle. He directs his weight into the angle blocker and is prepared to turn his back to the angle blocker. He goes to the ground with that side of his body and creates a pile in the running lane.

If the defensive lineman ever feels that the two blockers are beginning to drive him back, he must drop the side of his body nearest the angle block to the ground and turn sideways in between the two blockers. This maneuver causes the two offensive players to block each other. The angle blocker blocks the defensive lineman's back, and the drive blocker blocks the defensive lineman's front. His body is wedged between

Figure 7.7 Defeating a double team block: *(a)* the defensive linebacker confronts the drive block first; *(b)* then he drops the side nearest the angle blocker to direct his weight into the angle blocker.

a

b

the two blockers and the energy of the block lessens. In this position, it is almost impossible for the blockers to move the defensive lineman out of the hole.

Trap Block

In the previous blocks, the defensive lineman was blocked by one or two offensive linemen who were either in front of him or to his right or left. In his stance, he could see the blockers and react immediately to their blocks. In a trap block, none of the blockers in the defensive lineman's sight block him. If the defensive end is lined up in front of the offensive tackle and he sees the tackle and guard block to the inside, he immediately thinks the tight end is going to angle block. However, the tight end is not blocking the defensive end, he's blocking straight ahead on the linebacker. The instant the defensive end reads this play, he should think trap block and turn back to the inside toward the center. He attacks the line of scrimmage and tries to locate the trap blocker. He faces the blocker and moves toward him (figure 7.8).

Once the defensive lineman has turned his body toward the center of the field and located the blocker, he is in position to defeat the block. At the moment of contact, he brings his outside arm and forearm hard across the blocker's chest and face. He keeps his knees bent, his back straight, and his head up. His shoulder pads should be at the same height as the blocker's pads (figure 7.9). He redirects the blocker's body back into the hole.

Every defensive lineman must understand that he can and will be trapped. When playing in front of an offensive guard, he must stay alert for the guard or tackle on the other side of the center who may try to trap block him. The nose tackle lined up in front of the offensive center has a more difficult job. When the center or guards aren't blocking him, he must look to both the right and left, because either offensive tackle may be coming to trap block him.

When beating the trap block, the defensive lineman must remember that it will take longer for the blocker to get to him. He should stay on or just across the line of scrimmage and not go upfield. He must locate which offensive player is going to trap block and turn to face the blocker. He needs to stay low, keep his knees bent, his head up, and his back straight, and he must not stand up. He meets the blocker by bringing his outside arm across the blocker's chest and face. He turns the blocker and drives him back into the hole where the running back wants to go.

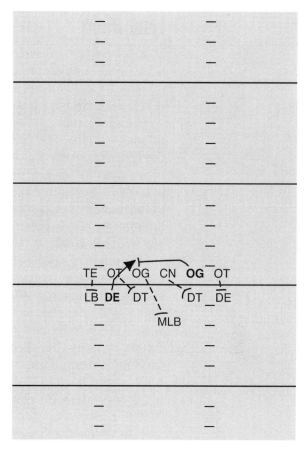

Figure 7.8 Trap block on the defensive end.

Figure 7.9 Defeating a trap block.

Lead Block

Many defensive linemen have trouble defeating the lead block. An offensive back, not an offensive lineman, executes this block. Like the trap block, the lead block does not happen the minute the ball is snapped. It takes time for the blocker to reach the defensive lineman.

The challenge comes when the defensive lineman who is not blocked by any offensive linemen begins to look into the backfield. Automatically his eyes seek out the ball carrier. He focuses on the running back with the ball and does not see the other running back coming in to block him from the side. The defensive lineman is usually bigger and stronger than the running back trying to block him. The blocker understands this, so he won't drive into the defensive lineman like an offensive lineman would. Instead, the blocker will try to block the defensive lineman at the hip with his shoulder pads.

Stopping this type of block is different because of the size of blocker and the method he uses to block the defensive lineman. To defeat the lead block, the defensive lineman must recognize that he is being blocked by a back and understand that it will take time for the blocker to reach him. He then has to locate the back who is going to block him. If necessary, he turns his body to face the blocker (figure 7.10a). He keeps his shoulder pads even with the blocker's shoulder pads. He stops the momentum of the block by hitting out with the palms of both hands, directing both palms into the top of the blocker's shoulder pads. He pushes the blocker's head, shoulders, and chest into the ground away from his own feet, legs, and body (figure 7.10b).

If the defensive lineman stands up and looks into the backfield for the ball carrier, the other running back will be into his body before he can react to the block. The defensive lineman needs to stay low and not help the blocker.

Lead blockers will attack any defensive lineman, so all defensive linemen should be prepared for running backs to try to block them. This block usually comes from a fullback who is lined up to one side of the center or directly behind the center and quarterback. The defensive lineman who is playing in front of the center must

Figure 7.10
Defeating a lead block: *(a)* defensive lineman turns to face the blocker; *(b)* defensive lineman pushes the blocker to the ground.

a

b

look out for a block from his outside by a fullback who may be lined up directly behind the offensive tackle.

Speed is essential in stopping a lead block. The defensive lineman must get rid of the blocker as quickly as possible. Good ball carriers understand that the running back will not be able to block for very long. Because of this, they often run right behind the blocker. The defensive lineman will have only a moment to push off the blocker, locate the ball carrier, and reach out to make the tackle.

Learning to defeat each type of block and understanding blocking progression is essential to becoming a top defensive lineman. As he continues to develop as a defensive lineman, he will be able to sit back, relax, close his eyes, and visualize how each block will come, who will do the blocking, and how he will defeat it.

RUSHING THE PASSER

There is nothing better for a defensive lineman than tackling a quarterback and getting a sack. When playing the defensive line against a running play, the defensive lineman reacts to the block being used by the offense. This changes when the offensive lineman sets up to pass block. Now the defensive player is in control. He is the one making the moves, while the offensive lineman has to react to the defensive lineman.

A pass rusher must anticipate when the offense is going to try to pass the ball. He adjusts his stance when he anticipates a pass and concentrates on the ball. He starts moving forward the instant the center moves the ball. Any time the defense thinks the offense is going to pass the ball, defensive linemen need to decide before the play begins what pass rush move they are going to use. They attack the target area and make the offensive blocker react to them. They pressure the passer, force the quarterback to hurry the throw, and bat or deflect any pass they can. They tackle the quarterback every chance they get.

The defensive lineman uses a balanced stance when defending a running play. He has a wide base and can react to his right or left. When the defensive lineman thinks the offense is going to pass, he changes his stance so he can rush the passer. He narrows the distance between his feet and moves one foot back, bringing the front foot directly under his hip. He places one hand on the ground in front of his helmet, shifting most of his weight to the front foot and the hand on the ground. He raises his hips above his shoulders and focuses his eyes on the ball. He thinks about exploding forward and coming up as he moves across the line.

Getting a sack is not the only way to defeat an offensive pass play. Making the quarterback move, or forcing the quarterback to leave the pocket, can cause a poor pass or at least force the pass to only half of the field. A defensive player can also rush the quarterback and force him to throw the ball before a receiver gets open. Another way to influence a pass play is for the defensive player to anticipate when the quarterback is going to throw and then reach up and deflect or redirect the ball. Any of these actions help a team defend the pass. Each action can result in an incompletion, which is just as good as stopping an offensive running play for no yards.

Defensive linemen use several pass-rush techniques. The key is to find the one or two that are best suited to the size of the individual player. Regardless of the technique, the defensive lineman must always have an idea of where the quarterback will set up to throw (the target area). He must remember that his ultimate goal is to influence the quarterback, but he needs to defeat the blocker first. He must keep moving forward and keep his legs and feet moving toward the quarterback. He needs to be aggressive for the entire play. If these movements become second nature to the defensive lineman and his feet, legs, hips, upper body, arms, and hands move together smoothly, he is on his way to becoming a great pass rusher.

Straight-Ahead Bull Rush

The first pass-rush technique is the straight-ahead bull rush. In this play, the defensive lineman quickly comes off the ball and drives forward to the target area, where the quarterback will set up to throw.

In this pass rush, the defensive lineman's goal is not to get around the blocker but to drive the offensive blocker right back into the quarterback. If he can drive the blocker into the quarterback, he can interrupt the quarterback's throwing motion and possibly force the quarterback to throw before he is ready, interrupting the pass timing. This type of rush is effective against a blocker who backs away from the line of scrimmage.

On the snap of the ball, the defensive lineman explodes off the line in a low charge (figure 7.11a). He keeps his shoulders below the blocker's shoulders and bends his arms, keeping his elbows close to his body. His palms are up with the fingers open and thumbs close together.

As the defensive lineman reaches the blocker, he drives the palms of his hands into the armpits of the blocker (figure 7.11b). He pushes his arms forward and up, raising the blocker up and back (figure 7.11c). He drives the blocker into the quarterback with short, quick steps, and he keeps driving until he reaches the quarterback, the pass is thrown, or the whistle blows.

a b c

Figure 7.11   Straight-ahead bull rush: *(a)* DL explodes off the line; *(b)* he makes contact with the blocker; *(c)* he pushes the blocker back toward the quarterback.

Bull and Jerk

This is a variation of the normal bull rush that should be taught right from the start. Often when the defensive lineman is successful pushing the blocker into the quarterback, the blocker sets his feet and lunges at the defensive lineman. The defensive lineman must be alert to this possibility as he charges at the blocker. It is important for the lineman to use the blocker's forward thrust to help pull the blocker out of the way.

When the defensive lineman sees the blocker set and lunge, he grabs the front of the blocker's jersey in both hands and jerks or pulls the blocker's body to the side (figure 7.12a). He steps across the blocker's body with the foot on the same side that he pulled the blocker to and drives past the blocker to the target area (figure 7.12b).

a   b

Figure 7.12   Bull and jerk: *(a)* DL grabs the blocker's jersey and jerks the blocker to the side; *(b)* DL continues to the target area.

Rushing to the Outside

There are two techniques for rushing to the outside shoulder of a blocker. The first works for a defensive lineman who is shorter than the offensive blocker. The second is helpful for a defensive lineman who is the same height as or taller than the offensive blocker.

The shoulder club and arm slip pass rush is an ideal pass-rush technique for a shorter player to learn and perfect. In this technique, the defensive lineman steps quickly with his inside foot, takes a long step with his outside foot, and gets in position to touch the blocker (figure 7.13a). He takes his outside hand and arm and hits hard under the blocker's shoulder pad, lifting his shoulder and arm up.

He steps to the outside of the blocker with his inside foot while dropping his inside shoulder and driving it under the armpit of the blocker. He bows and pushes back his neck and back. He drives his hips up and past the blocker and keeps moving to the quarterback (figure 7.13b).

The wrist-club and arm-over pass rush begins the same way. Instead of pushing the blocker's shoulder and arm up, now the defensive lineman directs them down and into the blocker's chest. As the defensive lineman's second step hits, he uses his outside forearm to drive down on the blocker's outside forearm and wrist (figure 7.14a). The defensive lineman drives the blocker's arm and hand down and into his chest. He reaches over the blocker's outside shoulder with his inside arm and drives his elbow into the blocker's back. He drives his inside leg to the outside and past the offensive blocker (figure 7.14b). He keeps moving forward and attacks the quarterback.

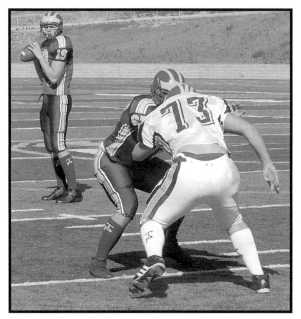

a   b

Figure 7.13 Shoulder club and arm slip pass rush: *(a)* defensive linebacker makes contact with the blocker; *(b)* he drives past the blocker to the quarterback.

Rushing to the Inside

The defensive lineman uses the rip and run pass rush technique to take an inside path to the quarterback. The defensive lineman attacks the inside of the offensive blocker with a rip and run. Often this uncovers the shortest and quickest path to the quarterback. This technique is unique in that the defensive lineman commits to an inside rush on the snap of the ball and only the rip arm comes in contact with the offensive blocker. The instant the center moves the ball, the defensive lineman takes a long step with his outside foot forward and across the blocker's body, allowing his outside shoulder to drop (figure 7.15a). The defensive lineman tries to drive his outside shoulder under the blocker's inside armpit. He propels himself past the blocker by bringing his outside arm up and back. He drives his feet and hips toward the quarterback (figure 7.15b).

a

b

Figure 7.14 Wrist-club and arm-over pass rush: *(a)* defensive linebacker pushes the blocker's arms down; *(b)* he moves past the blocker to the quarterback.

a

b

Figure 7.15 Rip and run pass rush: *(a)* DL drops his outside shoulder to get past the blocker; *(b)* he continues to the quarterback.

DEFENSIVE LINEMAN DRILLS

It is always a good idea for defensive linemen to practice getting off the ball and hitting with their shoulder pads and hands against a big bag or sled before they take on live offensive blockers. When working on any of these techniques, the defensive lineman can go through the motions without having an offensive player blocking him. Without a blocker, players can repeat the movement many times and won't become as fatigued or go through the pounding that comes with contact.

Instant Movement on the Ball

Purpose: To improve the reaction time of defensive linemen to the snap of the ball.

Procedure:

1. The coach lines up at the offensive center's position on one knee with a ball on the ground.
2. Defensive linemen move into their positions.
3. When the coach snaps the ball, the defensive linemen charge straight ahead.

Variations: This drill is also good for practicing control and crossover steps. To practice the control step, the coach calls out the direction of the first control step when he snaps the ball. To practice the crossover step, the coach calls out which foot to use in the crossover when he snaps the ball.

Coaching Points: When defensive linemen are practicing the start, it is important that someone makes a movement like the center snapping the ball. If the defensive lineman is charging straight ahead, he takes a quick forward step with his back foot, keeping his back straight, shoulders low and square, and his head and eyes up. The important thing is for him to attack the line of scrimmage.

Facing the Drive Block

Purpose: To give defensive linemen experience defeating the drive block.

Procedure:

1. The coach stands to the side of the defensive lineman. Another defensive lineman serves as the offensive blocker. He lines up opposite the defensive lineman. The coach tells the defensive player the side of main gap responsibility.
2. The coach calls out the snap count to start the drive. The blocker executes the drive block.
3. The defensive lineman reacts to the drive block.

Variation: This drill is good for working on the hook block as well. For the hook block, the defensive lineman serving as the blocker lines up to the side of the defensive lineman.

Coaching Points: The defensive player should move the instant the blocker starts forward. He should keep his shoulder pads below the blocker's pads. At contact, his head should slide to his gap responsibility, his arms should extend, and he should separate from the blocker. He should continue to drive the blocker for four or five steps until the coach blows a whistle.

Playing the Angle Block

Purpose: To give defensive linemen experience defeating the angle block.

Procedure:
1. The coach stands to the side of the defensive lineman. The defensive lineman sets up on the line and two offensive linemen line up, one in front of the defensive lineman and one to the side.
2. The coach calls out the snap count to start the drive.
3. The defensive lineman reacts to the angle block from the side. The offensive lineman who lined up opposite the defensive lineman is not blocking and can step to the inside.

Variations: This drill can also be used to work on the scoop block and the double team block. When working on the scoop block or the double team block, the offensive lineman who lines up opposite the defensive lineman does block. The defensive lineman must correctly defeat the block.

Coaching Points: The defensive player must start forward on the movement of the offensive blockers. He must lean into the angle block as it develops. Against the scoop block, he needs to direct his charge into the second blocker and push him back into the offensive backfield. Against a double team, he must play both blockers and go to the ground by dropping the side of his body nearest the angle blocker to keep from being driven off the line.

Blocker in the Hole

Purpose: To give defensive linemen experience defeating the trap block.

Procedure:
1. The coach lines up in the offensive backfield with an offensive lineman and a tight end (or another offensive lineman) and a trapping defensive lineman.
2. The coach calls the snap count to start the play. The offensive player in front of the defensive man blocks to the inside, the tight end blocks straight ahead, and the trapping lineman pulls and tries to trap the defensive player.
3. The defensive lineman sees and reacts to the trap block.

Variation: This drill also works for the lead block. For the lead block, an additional blocker sets up in the backfield and lead blocks the defensive lineman.

Coaching Points: Against a trap block, the defensive player should take short steps to protect against a drive or angle block. He then should stop his charge, look inside, and turn to face the trapping lineman. At contact, he should bring his outside forearm across the blocker's face and chest.

Attacking the Target Area

Purpose: To give the defensive lineman practice sprinting to where he thinks the quarterback will set up.

Procedure:

1. Place a shirt or dummy directly behind the ball 7 yards off the line of scrimmage to mark the target area. The coach stands behind the target area to observe the defensive linemen.
2. The defensive linemen form one line. The first defensive lineman gets into his normal stance on the line.
3. The defensive lineman can start the play on his own or can react to someone simulating the snap.
4. The defensive lineman takes a quick charge, running to the target area as fast as he can.

Coaching Points: When attacking the target area, defensive linemen should move from one side of the ball to the other. The defensive lineman should change his stance from a running defense stance to more of a pass-rush stance.

Once the defensive lineman is coming off the ball on the snap and attacking the target area, the coach can begin to teach the pass-rush techniques to defeat an offensive blocker. The coach should walk through each technique, making certain that player movements and steps are correct. Then players can speed up their movements in preparation for actual blockers.

Straight-Ahead Bull Rush

Purpose: To reinforce proper technique for a straight-ahead bull rush.

Procedure:

1. The coach stands to the side of the defensive lineman. The defensive lineman lines up in front of the offensive lineman, who is set up to pass protect.
2. On the coach's snap count, the defensive lineman rushes, using a straight-ahead bull rush to get past the offensive lineman.
3. The coach provides feedback.

Variations: This drill is useful for practicing other pass rush technique as well. For the bull and jerk, the offensive lineman lunges at the defensive lineman. For the shoulder club and arm slip pass rush and the wrist-club and arm-over pass rush, the defensive lineman lines up on the outside shoulder of the blocker. For the rip and run pass rush, the defensive man lines up directly in front of the blocker.

Coaching Points: In any pass rush drill the defensive lineman needs to move forward in a low charge on the snap and slowly come up as he nears the blocker. The drill should continue until the defensive man reaches the target area or the coach blows a whistle. The pass rusher or the coach should determine before the snap what rush technique to use.

Linebacker

Linebacker is one of the most difficult positions on the defensive side of the ball. On a single play, the linebacker may defeat a blocker, tackle the ball carrier, and stop a running play. On the next, he may have to read the pass play, react to his coverage assignment, and play pass defense.

Being a linebacker is demanding from both a physical and mental standpoint. There is a great deal for a linebacker to learn and do, but the position can be a lot of fun. Most linebackers have a real love of football and have fun both in practice and during the game. Often they set the tempo at practice, liven up drills, and make the practice time pass quickly.

Linebacker is a challenging position to learn, and players should not be discouraged if it is difficult at first. To be an outstanding linebacker, a player must use the proper stance, understand who can block him, move on the ball, defeat different kinds of blocks, drop into man-to-man coverage and zone coverage, and blitz to reach the quarterback.

STANCE

The linebacker's stance varies depending on where he plays, inside or outside. The initial stance must allow him to react to a wide variety of blocks and provide for easy movement into his pass defense responsibility. The stance used by a linebacker depends on the style of his team's defense. Both inside and outside linebackers should bend at the knees and not at the waist, keep the back straight, and keep the head up and eyes focused straight ahead.

An inside linebacker starts with his feet even and about shoulder-width apart, with the feet pointing straight ahead. He bends a little at the knees and brings his shoulders forward slightly, in front of his feet. Keeping his elbows in against his body, he lifts his forearms up and out so they extend in front of his body. His hands are open and his fingers are spread (figure 8.1).

An outside linebacker's stance is much like an inside linebacker's, but it varies depending on whether or not the outside linebacker has a blocker in front of him. When an outside linebacker lines up in front of an offensive tackle, he uses the same stance as an inside linebacker. When he lines up in front of a tight end, he moves his outside foot back slightly until it is even with the middle of his inside foot (figure 8.2a). He keeps his hands up to react to the tight end's block. An outside linebacker who has no one in front of him can drop his outside foot so that the toe is slightly behind the heel of his inside foot. When playing in this position, the outside linebacker can narrow his stance and allow his hands and arms to hang at his side in a relaxed manner (figure 8.2b). A linebacker should not change his stance when blitzing so that the offense won't be able to tell he is rushing until the ball is snapped.

Figure 8.1 Inside linebacker stance.

a   b

Figure 8.2   Outside linebacker stances: *(a)* lined up opposite a tight end; *(b)* lined up with no one in front.

MOVING ON THE BALL

The offense has the advantage of knowing when the play will start. To neutralize this advantage, the linebacker must concentrate on the ball and be prepared to move the instant the center begins the snap.

The linebacker position requires quick movement in many directions. A linebacker must move in a quick, decisive manner. Whether attacking straight ahead to defeat a blocker, coming on a blitz, moving in pursuit, or dropping for pass coverage, the linebacker needs to move with instant quickness. He must start moving with the snap of the ball.

Each move requires a different start. The body and mind become comfortable and respond to what is practiced, so it is important to learn the proper start and steps. When moving forward, the linebacker should step up with short, choppy, powerful steps that keep him balanced and allow him to aggressively engage an offensive blocker. He needs to practice the first step with both feet, as the foot used for the first step depends on the path of the blocker.

On a blitz, the linebacker rolls over the foot in the direction he is going and takes a quick step up with the other foot. An outside linebacker uses a long stride to cover a great deal of ground. For an inside linebacker, the first step is shorter so he can be ready to take on blockers. When moving in pursuit, the linebacker first takes a shuffle step in the direction he wants to go. He then slides his trailing foot until it is under his hips. The starting movement and steps must be quick and decisive.

When dropping into zone pass defense, the linebacker first takes a crossover step. The linebacker turns slightly, leans, and rolls over the foot in the direction he wants to go. He quickly steps with the opposite foot, bringing his foot and leg across his body. He should now be moving to his zone. When going into man-to-man coverage, the linebacker's first movement is a step back away from the line of scrimmage. He must keep his hips and shoulders square to the line of scrimmage. He can adjust his movement once the offensive blocker makes his move.

DEFEATING BLOCKS

Every defensive player must understand that he has to defeat at least one blocker before he will be in position to tackle the ball carrier. The first step to becoming a great linebacker is to know the order in which different blockers come. Some blockers get to the linebacker quickly, and he has to react instantly. Other blockers take longer to get to him, giving him time to position himself properly.

Blocking Progression

When linebackers know the order that blockers will come, it becomes much easier to stay calm and get into position to defeat the block and move to the ball carrier. They start by focusing on the first blocker, then they move from one blocker to the next in a relaxed, controlled progression. To understand block progression, linebackers must know in what order the blockers will come, what type of block each blocker will use, how to defeat each type of block, and how to locate the ball carrier and be part of the tackle.

Against any offensive running play, once the ball is snapped the linebacker must follow these actions in precise order. First, the linebacker determines who is trying to block him, and then he analyzes what type of block is going to be used. He defeats the block, locates the ball carrier, and makes the tackle. Against a run, a linebacker starts moving. Then he quickly determines who is going to block him, instantly attacks the blocker, and defeats the block.

Let's first look at the middle linebacker playing in front of the center. Most likely, the center is the first to attack the middle linebacker. Next, one of the offensive guards attacks the middle linebacker, most likely the guard opposite the direction of the center's block. Third, one of the offensive tackles blocks the middle linebacker, usually the tackle to the side of the backfield movement. Fourth, any lead back may block him, followed by the tight end. This is the middle linebacker's blocking progression (figure 8.3).

When an inside linebacker is playing in front of the offensive guard, the first blocker he must concentrate on is the guard. If the guard blocks to the inside on the nose tackle, the inside linebacker's next blocker is the offensive tackle to the linebacker's side. Following the offensive tackle, he needs to look to the guard from the other side of the formation, then any lead back, and finally the tight end to his side (figure 8.4).

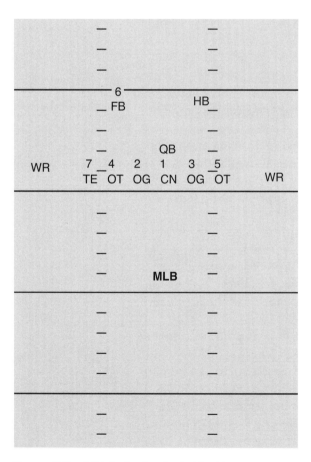

Figure 8.3 Middle linebacker's blocking progression.

An outside linebacker who is playing in front of an offensive tackle to the tight end side first looks to the offensive tackle. If the offensive tackle blocks to the inside or pulls to the outside and does not block the outside linebacker, the linebacker must locate the tight end. After the tight end, he looks for the offensive guard on his side, and then the near back who may be leading through the line. The final blocker is the offensive guard from the opposite side of the formation (figure 8.5).

An outside backer who lines up in front of an offensive tackle on the open side can eliminate the tight end as a blocker. The order of his blocking progression is the offensive tackle in front of him, then the offensive guard on his side, then an offensive back who can be a lead blocker, and finally the offensive guard from the other side of the offensive center.

For an outside linebacker who lines up in front of an offensive tight end, the tight end is his first blocker and the offensive tackle on his side is number two. The order of the rest of the blockers is the same as if he were playing in front of the offensive tackle (figure 8.6).

When playing in open space, the order of the blockers changes for an outside linebacker. The first blocker he needs to focus on is the offensive guard on his side. Next is any lead back lined up on his side, and then the offensive guard from the opposite side of the formation. In addition to these three blockers, he must know if he is facing a team that pulls the center to block on the linebacker or that may crack block on him with an outside wide receiver (figure 8.7).

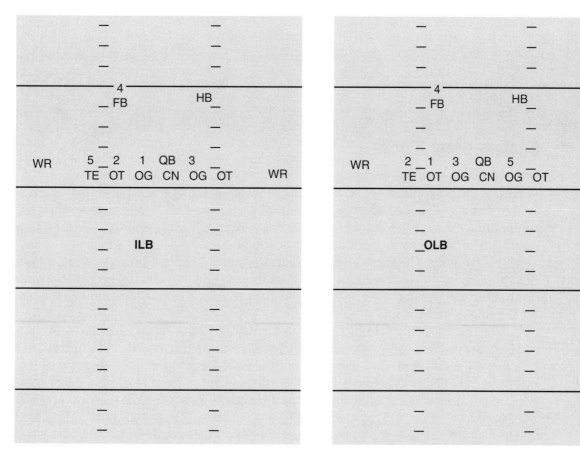

Figure 8.4 Inside linebacker's blocking progression.

Figure 8.5 Blocking progression for the outside linebacker on the tight end side.

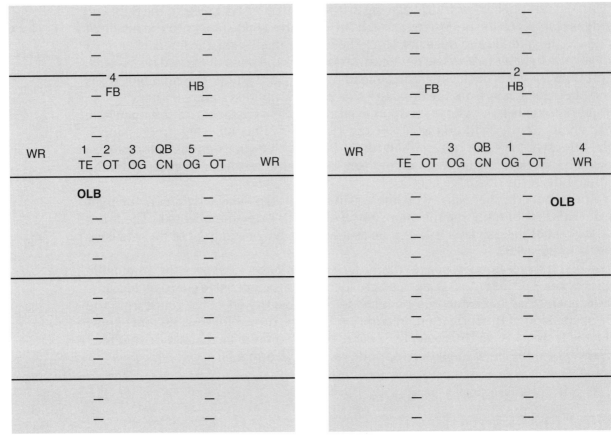

Figure 8.6 Blocking progression for an outside linebacker lined up in front of a tight end.

Figure 8.7 Blocking progression for an outside linebacker lined up with no one in front of him.

Beating Drive Blocks

A drive block on a linebacker comes from an offensive blocker lined up directly in front of the linebacker. The blocker comes straight at the linebacker and tries to drive the linebacker back off the line of scrimmage. The linebacker starts his momentum toward the blocker (figure 8.8a). He must have a wide base and take short, powerful steps to meet and defeat the block.

The linebacker should try to make first contact (figure 8.8b). He should keep his shoulder pads slightly below the blocker's shoulder pads. In this position, the linebacker will be able to keep the blocker from getting under him and driving him off the line of scrimmage.

Unless the linebacker is responsible for plugging the running lanes on both sides of the blocker (two-gap responsibility), he is responsible for one side of the drive blocker only. As he steps forward and his shoulder pads make contact with the offensive blocker, he slides his helmet to the side of his gap responsibility (figure 8.8c). The linebacker should use his pads, not his helmet, to make contact with the blocker.

The instant the linebacker's shoulder pads make contact, he extends his arms so the palms of both hands make contact at the numbers of the offensive blocker's jersey (figure 8.8d). He then straightens his arms, separates from the blocker, throws the blocker aside, and gets ready to attack the ball carrier.

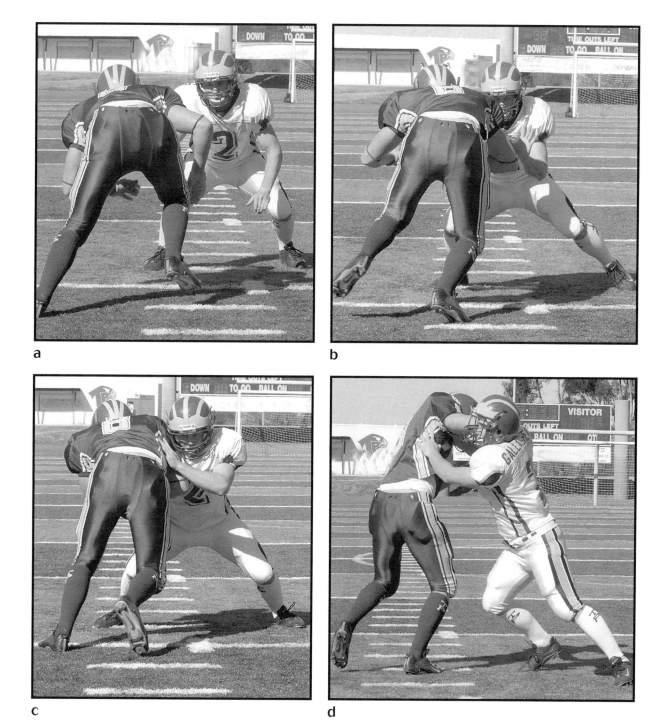

a   b

c   d

Figure 8.8 Defeating a drive block: *(a)* linebacker takes short, powerful steps toward the blocker; *(b)* he makes contact with his shoulder pads; *(c)* he slides his helmet to the side of his gap responsibility; *(d)* he separates from the blocker.

If the linebacker is blitzing through a gap, he moves directly to one side of the blocker on the snap of the ball. In a blitz defense, it is important for the linebacker to fight back into the blocker and not let the blocker use the linebacker's own momentum to drive him out of the hole.

Beating Hook Blocks

An outside linebacker has to face and defeat hook blocks. A tight end often uses this block on wide running plays to his side. The tight end's objective when using the hook block is to block the linebacker's penetration across the line and stop him from moving to the right or left down the line of scrimmage. Tight ends are more agile than offensive linemen and they move with greater quickness. The hook block does not require a great deal of power, instead relying on the speed of the blocker to get into position on the defensive linebacker.

Defeating this block starts with understanding the block progression. First, the linebacker's focus is on the tight end lined up directly in front of him. His focus stays on the tight end until he is certain the tight end is not attacking him.

Recognition of the block is the key to stopping it. When the play begins, the linebacker will see the tight end move laterally rather than directly at the linebacker. The tight end will try to get into a position in which his helmet is outside the linebacker's shoulder pad so he can drive his shoulder away from his movement into the linebacker's belly and hip. As the linebacker takes his first, short step forward, he sees the tight end's helmet and shoulder pads move laterally. He quickly extends both arms into the tight end, trying to make contact with the palms of both hands on the front portion of the tight end's shoulder pads (figure 8.9a).

If he extends his hands and arms into the tight end quickly enough, the linebacker will have the greater power at the moment of contact. The tight end's momentum may still be lateral rather than forward (figure 8.9b). As the linebacker's hands make contact, he continues to take short power steps and drives the tight end back across the line of scrimmage into the offensive backfield. In this position, the linebacker is able to control the tight end, preventing him from using his shoulder pads to get into the linebacker's legs or body. Once the tight end is under control, the linebacker should look up and locate the ball carrier. Based on the path of the ball carrier, the linebacker will know the direction he wants to move. He sheds the blocker in the opposite direction (figure 8.9c) and quickly moves to get in on the tackle.

Beating Angle Blocks

All linebackers need to learn to recognize the angle block as quickly as possible. This block is used mostly against inside linebackers, but it can also be used against outside linebackers. The outside linebacker who lines up in front of the tight end may be angle blocked by a wing back who blocks from the outside or by an offensive tackle blocking from the inside.

The instant the offensive player lined up in front of the linebacker blocks to one side, the linebacker should be alert for an angle block. The angle block will come from the opposite side of the blocker's movement directly in front of the linebacker. If the blocker in front of the linebacker moves right, the angle blocker will come from the left. This block comes the instant the ball is snapped. Usually the linebacker does not have the time to turn and face the blocker that he does when defeating a drive or hook block.

As he sees the angle blocker moving toward him, the linebacker quickly steps at the blocker with the foot on the same side as the block (figure 8.10a). He meets the blocker with the shoulder pad on that side. As the shoulder pad makes contact, the linebacker strikes with his arm and forearm. He leans into the blocker to stop the blocker's momentum. He drives the palm of his other hand into the blocker's shoulder pad and attempts to knock the blocker off balance, pushing him back to where the ball carrier wants to run (figure 8.10b).

a

Figure 8.9 Defeating a hook block: *(a)* linebacker extends his arms and pushes the tight end; *(b)* tight end's momentum is lateral; *(c)* the linebacker sheds the tight end and pursues the ball carrier.

b

c

The linebacker's goal is to hold his ground and not let the offensive blocker drive him off the line of scrimmage. The quicker he reacts to the block, the faster he can stop the blocker's momentum. If the linebacker can create a pile using himself and the angle blocker, the running back will be forced to run somewhere else where other defensive players can make the tackle.

Beating Trap Blocks

Both inside and outside linebackers must be prepared to face the trap block. This block does not come at the linebacker the instant the ball is snapped. It takes time for the play to develop and for the blocker to get to the linebacker.

a

Figure 8.10 Defeating an angle block: *(a)* LB steps toward the blocker; *(b)* he drives the blocker into the hole.

b

Usually the trap blocker is at least two players removed from the linebacker when he lines up. For an outside linebacker, the trap blocker is either offensive guard. For an inside linebacker, the trap blocker is the guard or tackle on the other side of the offensive center. If neither the guard nor tackle comes to trap block, the inside linebacker should immediately look to the outside for the tight end. The trap block may come from the outside on the tight end's side of the ball.

The trap blocker's goal is to knock the linebacker out of the hole, creating a path for the ball carrier. The trap blocker counts on two things to happen. First, he hopes the linebacker will come across the line of scrimmage. Second, he hopes the linebacker's focus will be on the ball carrier and, therefore, the linebacker will not see the trap blocker coming to block. The trap blocker will come with momentum so it is essential for the linebacker to brace himself for the block (figure 8.11a). His reaction must be quick and decisive. He turns to face the blocker (figure 8.11b). He bends his knees and brings his outside shoulder and forearm across the blocker's helmet and chest. He pushes the blocker into the hole and uses his body to block the running lane (figure 8.11c).

For the inside linebacker, the read is different. The inside linebacker's first read is the offensive player in front of him. If the offensive player blocks to his left, the inside linebacker looks at the offensive player to his left to make sure he is not angle blocking him. If neither offensive player blocks him, he looks for the trap block.

The inside linebacker's first response is to attack toward the offensive side of the ball. As the inside linebacker comes up, he looks across the center to the other side of the ball to try to determine if the guard or tackle is trying to trap block him. Once he determines who the blocker is, the linebacker slows his forward movement and prepares to attack the blocker. When taking on the trap blocker, he uses the

a

b

c

Figure 8.11 Defeating a trap block: *(a)* linebacker braces himself for contact with the trap blocker; *(b)* he turns to face the blocker; *(c)* he pushes the blocker into the running lane.

same technique as the outside linebacker, bringing his outside forearm across the blocker's helmet with as much force as he can. The goal is to put the blocker into the ball carrier's running lane.

Both outside and inside linebackers must remember to keep their shoulders even with the blocker's pads. The linebacker's head must be up, his back straight, and his knees bent. He explodes into the blocker with the large muscles of the legs and with his forearm.

Beating Lead Blocks

All the blocks so far have come from either an offensive lineman or a tight end. The lead block is different because the running back is the potential blocker. Both inside and outside linebackers must be prepared to take on the running back's block. A running back may not have the bulk or strength found in most offensive linemen and some tight ends, but he will have quickness and explosive power, which he can incorporate into the block.

Often a bigger back, such as a fullback who is used as a lead blocker, may come at the linebacker with the same technique an offensive lineman uses on a trap or running drive block. Because of their size, smaller, quicker backs may hesitate to hit a linebacker high and will instead try to block the linebacker at the hip.

When a linebacker looks into the backfield, he often focuses on the man with the ball. The running back assigned to block him is counting on that—he wants the linebacker's concentration on the ball carrier and not on him. For this reason, the linebacker needs to focus on the blocker. Before the snap of the ball, the linebacker should locate the position of any running back who is a potential blocker. He concentrates on the man in front of him, but it helps a great deal to know that the possibility of a block by a running back does exist.

When a running back lines up behind the offensive tackle to the outside linebacker's side, the outside linebacker must be aware that he could be a possible blocker. An inside linebacker must be alert for the possibility of a lead block when he sees any I or offset I formations. In either case, the linebacker must locate the running back the instant he determines he is not being blocked by an offensive lineman or tight end. When he sees the back coming at him, the linebacker must move forward to meet the blocker at the line of scrimmage.

If the running back is coming high, the linebacker can play the blocker as he would play a trap block. An outside linebacker can bring his outside arm across the blocker's head and shoulders and force the blocker's body into the hole where the ball carrier wants to run. When a running back comes at the linebacker high, the linebacker needs to keep his head on the side of his gap responsibility. He must always play to one-half of the lead blocker in order to quickly get off the block and make the tackle. He can use the forearm and shoulder away from his gap responsibility to deliver a blow on the running back if the running back tries to block the linebacker high.

If the running back's shoulders start to dip and angle to the ground, the linebacker should recognize this as a sign that the running back will try to block him at his hip. The linebacker should extend both hands hard into the top of the running back's shoulder pads. As the linebacker pushes the blocker's head and shoulders down into the ground, he straightens his arms, keeping both his feet and legs away from the blocker. An inside linebacker plays the lead block the same way, using his hands and arms to keep the blocker away from his legs.

BLITZING

Rushing across the line of scrimmage to blitz the quarterback or ball carrier is a tremendous amount of fun for a linebacker. This is the time he gets to be the aggressor and go after the quarterback or the ball carrier instead of reacting to offensive blocks or dropping into pass coverage.

A linebacker may run a blitz when the offense runs or passes the ball. When attacking the line of scrimmage against a running play, he should use the same block progression reads that he uses from his normal alignment. With the momentum of the blitz, he should use the same techniques to defeat the various blocks. Blitzing against a running play can disrupt the blocking of the play, forcing the ball carrier to alter his path and often resulting in a tackle for a loss on the offensive side of the ball.

Blitzing linebackers must understand that getting a sack is not the only way to defeat an offensive pass play. Forcing the quarterback to leave the pocket and run can cause a poor pass or at least force the pass into only one-half of the field. Or, sometimes the quarterback is rushed but does not run, forcing the throw before the receiver comes open. Another way to influence a pass play is to anticipate when the quarterback is going to throw the ball. As the quarterback starts to throw, the linebacker stretches his arms up to deflect or redirect the ball. All three instances can result in a successful pass defense.

Blitzing means the roles are reversed. When a linebacker plays against a running play, he must react to the block being used by the offense. This changes when the offensive lineman or running back sets up to pass block and the linebacker is on a blitz. Now the linebacker is the one making the moves and the offensive blocker is put in the position of reacting to what the linebacker decides to do. The linebacker needs to anticipate when the offense is going to try to pass the ball as he gets ready to blitz. He concentrates on the ball and starts moving forward the instant the center moves the ball. He determines and defeats the offensive pass blocker and then accelerates to the quarterback.

Before working on pass-rush technique, the linebacker should work on getting off and sprinting to the target area, the place he thinks the quarterback will set up. When practicing attacking the target area, the linebacker should rush from both sides of the ball. Once he is coming off the ball on the snap and attacking the target area, he can begin to learn pass-rush techniques to defeat offensive blockers. The linebacker should walk through each technique, making certain his movements and steps are correct. Once he has the correct form, he can speed up his movements in preparation for working against an actual blocker.

When coming on a blitz, the linebacker must be prepared to be blocked by a big offensive lineman or a smaller offensive back. The linebacker should try to determine immediately who is assigned to block him as he moves on the snap of the ball. He must focus on defeating the blocker before going after the quarterback or the ball carrier.

When the Running Back Blocks

When the linebacker sees a running back has been assigned to block him on a pass play, he should determine how to defeat the running back. If the running back is shorter, one of the most effective ways to get around him is the arm-over technique.

The linebacker immediately squares himself with his blocker, turning his chest to face the blocker's chest. He takes a short inside step and moves his head to the inside (fakes) when he is two steps away from the blocker. The linebacker uses his outside arm and hand to hit the blocker's shoulder pads, driving his shoulder and arm toward the blocker's chest. The linebacker steps to the outside and brings his inside arm up and over the blocker's shoulder. He drives his elbow into the blocker's back and sprints past the blocker to the quarterback.

The goal of the bull rush is not to get around the blocker, it is to drive the blocker back into the quarterback. By forcing the blocker into the quarterback, the linebacker interrupts the quarterback's throwing motion, possibly forcing the quarterback to throw before he is ready. As the linebacker reaches the blocker, he drives the palms of both hands into the blocker's armpits (figure 8.12a). He pushes his arms forward and up, raising the blocker up and back. He uses short, quick steps to drive the blocker back into the quarterback (figure 8.12b). The linebacker keeps driving the blocker back until he reaches the quarterback or the whistle blows. This type of rush is very effective against a running back who backs up toward the quarterback and never gets set to stop the charge.

The bull and jerk rush is a variation of the normal bull rush and should be practiced right from the start. If the linebacker is successful pushing the blocker into the quarterback, the blocker may set his feet and try to lunge or fire out at the linebacker. The linebacker must be ready for this as he charges straight at the blocker, using the blocker's forward thrust to pull the blocker out of the way. When the

a   b

Figure 8.12 Bull rush technique: *(a)* linebacker makes contact with his hands; *(b)* he drives the blocker back into the quarterback.

linebacker sees the blocker set and his chest and helmet come at the linebacker, the linebacker grabs the front of the blocker's jersey in both hands (figure 8.13a). He jerks or pulls the blocker's body to one side (figure 8.13b). He steps across the blocker's body with the foot on the same side as the jerk and drives past the blocker to the target area (figure 8.13c).

a

b

c

Figure 8.13 Bull and jerk: *(a)* linebacker grabs blocker's jersey as blocker lunges; *(b)* he jerks the blocker to one side; *(c)* he moves past the blocker to the quarterback.

When an Offensive Lineman Blocks

If an inside linebacker is going to blitz directly over an offensive guard, or an outside linebacker sees an offensive lineman moving out to block him, they must be ready to get around these bigger players to reach the quarterback.

If the guard is the same height or shorter, the linebacker can use the same arm-over blitz technique already covered (pages 145-146). The arm-over technique is more difficult to complete if the offensive blocker is taller than the linebacker. When going against a taller offensive blocker, the linebacker may want to use the arm-under blitz technique. This is an ideal pass rush technique for a shorter player to learn and perfect. The linebacker steps quickly with his inside foot. He takes a long step with his outside foot, putting himself in position to touch the blocker (figure 8.14a). He uses his outside hand and arm to hit hard into the under part of the blocker's shoulder pad, lifting the blocker's shoulder and arm (figure 8.14b). The linebacker steps to the outside of the blocker with his inside foot and drops his inside shoulder, driving it under the blocker's outside armpit. The linebacker pushes back, or bows, the blocker's neck and back. He drives his hips up and past the blocker and keeps moving to the quarterback (figure 8.14c).

a

b

c

Figure 8.14 Arm-under blitz technique: *(a)* linebacker hits under the blocker's shoulder pad; *(b)* he lifts the blocker's shoulder and arm; *(c)* he drives past the blocker to the quarterback.

MAN-TO-MAN COVERAGE

When asked to cover a receiver man-to-man, usually the linebacker covers a running back coming out of the offensive backfield. The linebacker begins 7 to 8 yards away from the man he is assigned to cover. Often he covers the running back all by himself, but sometimes he and another linebacker will work together to cover the running back. Man-to-man coverage requires great concentration, good technique, and an understanding of what the running back may do in order to get open.

In man-to-man coverage a linebacker backpedals, adjusts his backward run from a straight line to an angle (angle backpedal), leaves his backward run without losing momentum (rolling over), and recognizes the pass pattern being run by the running back. Once he learns these four techniques, the linebacker is ready to line up and cover any offensive back as he comes running out of the backfield to catch the ball.

For successful man-to-man coverage, the linebacker needs to use proper technique, recognize pass routes, roll over the foot in the direction of the coverage, and sprint to the running back. He must look back for the ball only when he can touch the running back and is in position to see the running back and the ball at the same time. He keeps his body between the receiver and his goal line. If the receiver does make the catch, the linebacker must be in position to make the tackle.

Footwork

For the backpedal, the linebacker begins in his normal stance. He pushes off his inside foot and steps back with his outside foot to begin the backpedal (figure 8.15). After taking the first step, he narrows the distance between his feet to no more than hip-width apart. He leans forward slightly with his shoulders just ahead of his hips. He allows his hands and arms to swing in normal running motion. With each step, he reaches back and does not push his body with his feet. He continues running in this manner for 10 yards.

Not every running back is going to run straight down the field. To get around the offensive linemen, the running back will have to release out of the backfield at an angle. The linebacker must adjust his backpedal to mirror the action of the running back. If the running back angles to the outside, the linebacker needs to backpedal at an angle to the outside. When the running back angles to the inside, the linebacker must do the same.

When changing the angle of the backpedal, the linebacker must not cross his feet. He must keep a smooth backward run and keep his head and shoulders in front of his hips. After backpedaling straight back for 5 yards, the linebacker angles to his left by swinging his right leg around to change direction. To return to a straight backpedal, he swings his left leg around to change direction. To angle backpedal to the right, he changes the direction of his backpedal by swinging his left leg back and around.

During any pass play in which the linebacker is in man-to-man coverage, he may need to leave the backward run. This occurs

Figure 8.15 Backpedal.

when he recognizes the pass route being run by the back or when the back gets within 3 yards of him. Going from a backward run to a forward run is a vital part of man-to-man coverage. The key is to maintain momentum, keeping the feet under the hips and always rolling over the foot in the direction the linebacker desires to go. Learning this skill plus exactly what path to take to get to the interception point will make him a much better defensive linebacker.

The linebacker leaves his backward run, quickly changing into a forward run at a 45-degree angle. To angle left, he leans his upper body back and to the left, rolling over his left foot. As he leans, his shoulders turn to the left. He will feel his right foot come across the front of his body as he continues to run.

When the linebacker rolls over his foot in the direction he wants to go, he maintains his momentum and will be able to run at top speed. He keeps both feet directly under his hips, allowing him to adjust to any double move pass routes, such as a corner pattern.

Recognizing Pass Routes

Once the linebacker can backpedal, angle backpedal, and roll over with ease, it is time to learn to recognize pass routes. He starts by learning the three areas on the field in which different pass routes will be run. The short zone is up to 6 yards from the line of scrimmage, the medium zone is from 7 to 12 yards, and the deep zone is more than 12 yards.

It will help the linebacker to think in terms of the three zones. When the running back is in the short zone, the linebacker only has to think about the pass routes the back can run in that area. As the running back moves to the medium zone, the linebacker looks only for medium routes. Once the running back goes past the medium zone, the focus is on deep pass routes.

There are three basic patterns that the running back will run in the short zone. The flat and wide routes are run to the outside. The angle route brings the running back across the center of the field. (See figure 4.13, page 75.) In the medium zone, the running back may run a stop route, usually at 7 yards, or an in or out route at 10 yards. (See figure 4.14, page 76.) In the deep zone, the running back can run a flat and up route, seam, post, or fan pass route. For any linebacker, these four pass routes are the most difficult to cover. The linebacker has to run farther, the ball is in the air longer, and the offense has a chance for a long gain. (See figure 4.15, page 77.)

When covering man-to-man, the linebacker must stay to one side of the running back as the running back comes down the field. If an inside linebacker is covering the running back by himself, he should try to keep his outside shoulder even with the running back's inside shoulder. An outside linebacker is in the opposite position—his inside shoulder should be even with the running back's outside shoulder. If the linebacker gets directly in front of the running back, the running back will be able to cut either way without trouble.

When playing man-to-man coverage, it is important to remember that an incompletion is just as good as stopping a running play for no gain. The linebacker should never take himself out of coverage by trying to guess the pass route, reaching behind the receiver to deflect the ball with only one hand, or looking back for the ball for an interception. He must stay with the running back and make interceptions when he is certain that he can make the catch.

ZONE COVERAGE

Playing zone pass defense is the opposite of playing man-to-man pass defense. In man-to-man, the focus is on the running back. The linebacker allows the receiver to tell him where to go by the pass route that is run, and the linebacker runs all over the field to cover the receiver for the entire length of the play. In zone defense, the linebacker is assigned to a specific area of the field. This is his area, and he reacts to any pass thrown in that area regardless of who is trying to make the catch. When playing zone defense, the linebacker must recognize the pass play, go immediately to his zone, get as deep in his zone as he can before the quarterback sets to throw, focus on the quarterback and the ball, and react to the pass, letting the ball direct the linebacker to the receiver.

First, the linebacker should learn the zones he will cover. The coach should outline the names and zones that will be used in the defense. On each zone pass defense, the linebacker is assigned one of the zones. Figure 8.16 shows one way to divide the medium zones on the field.

The technique the linebacker uses to drop into his zone depends on how wide he has to go from his original position to get into the zone. The wider he has to go, the more he will have to sprint. When he sprints, the linebacker rolls over the foot in the direction he needs to go and runs as fast as he can to his area. He should constantly look back over his shoulder to the quarterback.

Once he reaches his zone, he swings his inside leg around and begins to backpedal. As he starts to backpedal, he focuses on the quarterback. When he sees the quarterback is ready to throw, he stops his backpedal but keeps running in place, moving his feet in short, choppy steps. He prepares to move to either his right or left once he sees the quarterback start to throw. The linebacker breaks to the ball by rolling over the foot in the direction he needs to go.

One challenge a linebacker faces when playing zone defense is keeping his eyes on the quarterback and not looking at a receiver running into his zone. The linebacker will want to come up to cover the receiver before the ball is thrown, but he must resist this. He must practice going to his zone, looking at the quarterback, backpedaling, and then reacting to the right or left based on the throw. He should let the quarterback and the ball take him to the receiver. Focusing on the quarterback and the ball gives him a great chance to make an interception.

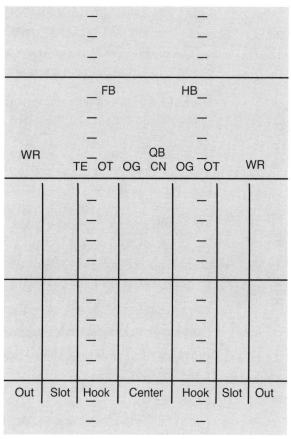

Figure 8.16 Zone coverage in the medium zone.

LINEBACKER DRILLS

It is a good idea to practice getting off the ball and hitting with the shoulder pads and hands against a big bag or sled before taking on offensive blockers. Of course, a bag or sled does not attack the way an offensive lineman will.

Starting Forward to the Blocker

Purpose: To improve quickness getting off with the snap.

Procedure:

1. The coach sets up at the center's position on one knee with a ball on the ground. Linebackers line up in their normal alignment on the defensive side of the line of scrimmage.
2. When the coach moves the ball, the linebacker moves.
3. This drill is good for fine-tuning starts from many different positions.

Variations: This drill is also good for practicing starting on a blitz. The coach should clearly define the start they are working on. To use the drill to practice starting in pursuit moving laterally to the ball carrier, the setup is the same except that the coach calls out the direction of the pursuit after moving the ball. To practice starting when dropping into zone coverage, the setup is the same except that the coach raises the ball into the air to alert the linebacker to drop. To practice starting when dropping into man-to-man coverage, the setup is the same except the coach calls out man coverage before moving the ball.

Coaching Points: Players should go one at a time. They should line up in their normal stance before the movement of the ball. The focus is on the first two or three steps of each movement.

Beating the Drive Block

Purpose: To reinforce proper technique when defeating the drive block and shedding the blocker.

Procedure:

1. The coach stands to the side of the linebacker. Another linebacker serves as the blocker.
2. To start the drill, the coach calls out the snap count and the backer's gap responsibility.
3. On the snap, the linebacker moves to defeat the drive block. Run the drill at half speed at first. Increase the tempo as the defensive man masters the proper technique.

Coaching Points: The linebacker needs to move forward to meet the blocker. His head should always end up on the side of his gap responsibility.

Defeating the Hook Block

Purpose: To reinforce proper technique when defeating a hook block and separating from the blocker.

Procedure:

1. The coach stands to the side of the outside linebacker. The outside linebacker lines up in front of a player in the tight end position. Another outside linebacker can serve as the tight end.
2. The coach calls out the snap count to start the drill.
3. On the snap, the linebacker moves to defeat the hook block.

Coaching Points: Begin the drill at half speed, then work up to full speed. The linebacker needs to get both hands on the blocker while he is still moving laterally.

Defeating the Angle Block

Purpose: To reinforce proper technique for defeating the angle block.

Procedure:

1. The coach lines up to the side of the linebacker. The linebacker and two offensive linemen get into position at the line of scrimmage.
2. The coach calls the snap count to start the play.
3. The linebacker should look at the offensive lineman in front of him and react to the angle block.

Coaching Points: The backer must step at the angle blocker and lean into his block. The hand opposite the block needs to be driven into the shoulder pad of the blocker to knock him off balance. Initially the drill should be run at half speed.

Defeating the Trap Block

Purpose: To reinforce proper technique for defeating the trap block and escaping the blocker.

Procedure:

1. The coach lines up in the offensive backfield with a tight end or offensive lineman and a trap blocker on the other side of the formation. Always have an offensive blocker directly in front of the linebacker. The trap blocker comes from the opposite side of the formation.
2. Each linebacker lines up in his position.
3. The coach calls the snap count to start the play.
4. Each linebacker reads the man in front of him blocking to the inside and then reacts to the trap block.

Variations: Inside linebackers can also use this drill to practice reading blocks and looking for the blocker. To use this drill to practice defeating the lead blocker, the setup is the same except another blocker is added to the backfield. This second blocker lead blocks the linebacker.

Coaching Points: The linebacker should turn to face the trap or lead blocker. Make sure that he attacks the blocker and does not sit and wait. Run the drill at half speed until the linebacker has the proper technique.

Finding the Target Area

Purpose: To train blitzing linebackers to go to the target area.

Procedure:

1. Place a shirt or dummy directly behind the ball 7 yards off the line of scrimmage.
2. The coach lines up on the offensive side behind the target area. The linebacker lines up in his normal stance.
3. To start the drill, the linebacker moves on his own or someone simulates the snap.
4. The linebacker takes a quick charge and runs to the target area as fast as he can.

Coaching Points: The backer must take a forward step as he starts his blitz. He should stay low on his charge and attack the target area as quickly as he can.

Arm-Over Rush

Purpose: To teach proper arm-over rushing technique.

Procedure:

1. The coach sets up outside the linebacker, even with the running back.
2. On the coach's signal, the linebacker pass rushes. The running back moves to block the rush.
3. The linebacker uses the arm-over technique to get past the running back and to the quarterback area.

Variations: This drill is also helpful for practicing bull rush technique against a running back. When using the drill to practice the bull and jerk rush, the running back lunges on the block. To practice the arm-under blitz technique, an offensive lineman sets up to block the linebacker.

Coaching Points: Both inside and outside linebackers should participate in this drill and practice blitzing from both sides of the ball. Begin the drill at half speed and then increase the tempo as the linebacker masters the technique.

Backpedaling

Purpose: To practice proper footwork when backpedaling.

Procedure:

1. The coach lines up in front of the linebacker.
2. On the coach's command, the linebacker starts to backpedal.
3. To practice angle backpedaling, the coach points for a change in direction as the linebacker moves back.

Coaching Points: The linebacker should step back with each step, keeping his shoulders in front of his hips and swinging his arms in a normal manner. When changing to an angle backpedal, he should not cross his feet.

Rolling Over

Purpose: To give linebackers a sense of what it feels like when they roll over.

Procedure:
1. The linebacker stands on the sideline, facing the field. His feet are even and hip-width apart.
2. Without turning his body, the linebacker leans his head, shoulders, and upper body to the right.
3. As his body moves over his right foot, he will feel his left leg automatically come across the front of his body. He takes a step in the direction of the lean.
4. Do the same drill leaning and rolling over the left foot.

Variation: To practice rolling over on the move, the coach points out the direction for the linebacker to roll over.

Coaching Points: Make certain the linebacker rolls over the foot in the direction he is to go and that he starts the movement by leaning his upper body.

Backward to Forward Run

Purpose: To practice switching from a backpedal to a forward run.

Procedure:
1. The linebacker lines up on the line of scrimmage.
2. The coach calls the snap count to start the play. The linebacker backpedals into his coverage. He begins his backward run at half speed.
3. At 10 yards, the linebacker leaves his backward run and quickly changes to a forward run at a 45-degree angle deep to his left. He leans his upper body back and to the left, rolling over his left foot. As he leans, his shoulders turn to the left.
4. His right foot comes across the front of his body as he continues to run.
5. He rolls over to his right.

Coaching Points: When the linebacker is comfortable rolling deep to his left and right, he can gradually increase the speed of his backward run. He should keep his momentum throughout the drill with his feet always under his hips.

Learning Pass Routes

Purpose: To learn to recognize pass routes.

Procedure:
1. The coach lines up with an offensive back. The linebacker gets into position.
2. On the coach's signal, the offensive back runs the pass route called by the coach.
3. The linebacker backpedals and calls out the pass route.

Coaching Points: The linebacker should stay on the proper side of the running back during the drill but not react. Do not use a ball during the drill.

Pointing Out and Calling Pass Patterns

Purpose: To train linebackers to concentrate on the running back, to learn pass routes, and to know where to go in coverage.

Procedure:

1. The linebacker gets into position on the line of scrimmage. A teammate lines up on the offensive side of the ball.
2. On the coach's signal, the linebacker starts to backpedal into coverage as his teammate begins to run a pass route at half speed.
3. The instant he recognizes the pass route, the linebacker points it out and calls out the name of the pass pattern. He keeps backpedaling while calling out the name.

Variation: To practice getting in good position to cover, the linebacker drives at the receiver once he calls out the pattern.

Coaching Points:

The backer should call and then point out where he should go to make his coverage. Once he is successful at this, the drill can change. The linebacker reacts to the pass route by rolling over and by driving to the running back. He should stay between the back and his own goal line.

Moving to Zone Coverage

Purpose: To reinforce proper zone coverage technique.

Procedure:

1. The coach lines up as a quarterback with the ball.
2. Facing the linebacker, the coach calls out the zone for the linebacker to drop into.
3. The coach calls "Hut" to start the drill.
4. The coach raises the ball as if to pass and the backer stops his drop.
5. The coach then steps and goes through the pass motion, causing the backer to react.
6. Once the linebacker is dropping, setting up, and reacting to the throwing motion, the coach can throw the ball to give the linebacker practice intercepting the pass.

Coaching Points: The backer should sprint to his zone and then backpedal to get set. The backer must focus on the coach and the ball. Do not use a receiver in the drill.

Defensive Back

Defensive back is one of the most exciting positions on the football team. The position requires a positive but not cocky attitude. The defensive back should be ready to make a touchdown-saving tackle, deflect a long pass at the last moment, or best of all, make an interception.

Successful defensive backs can't wait for the next play to begin. Ready to compete, they are eager to match their skill against the skill of the offensive player. The defensive back's off-season conditioning program should prepare him physically to run for the entire course of the game. In addition to physical stamina, this position requires mental toughness.

The skills a defensive back needs are the proper stance, the ability to move quickly on the snap and backpedal, knowledge and recognition of pass patterns, the ability to play zone and man-to-man coverage, and the ability to play the run.

STANCE AND START

The defensive backfield is the only defensive area on the football field in which the player's first movement is backward, not forward. The defensive back must be able to move backward at the speed of the receiver driving off the line. His beginning stance must allow him to explode into a backward run. If the defensive back does not have a specific man to cover, he may have the luxury of adjusting his stance.

Playing on the outside as a corner requires discipline. The corner gets into his stance by turning his front foot to the inside until he can feel his weight on the outside edge of the foot. Enough weight should be on the front foot to easily lift the back foot. At this point, he is in a position to use the larger muscles in the front of the lower leg, not just his toes, to push back when he starts. He then leans forward with his shoulders and lets his arms hang in a relaxed manner. His shoulders should be slightly in front of his forward foot. He keeps his shoulders even, his back straight, and his head and eyes up (figure 9.1a).

An inside strong safety can stand more erect. This gives him a good view of the entire offensive backfield. Depending on the coverage, the inside strong safety usually can bring his outside foot straight up instead of to the center of his body under his nose (figure 9.1b). A free safety has the freedom to line up with his feet even and spread comfortably apart (figure 9.1c). He can stand erect with only a slight forward lean of his shoulders. He needs to be able to see the entire field. Both the strong and free safety can learn the corner stance, especially if they might ever be asked to cover man-to-man on an inside wide receiver or play as a corner.

Every position on the team has its own specific skills. For a defensive back, the ability to start properly is crucial. From the start, he must move with the same speed and quickness as the wide receiver. When observing any top defensive back in a game, the speed and quickness they use in starting each and every play is evident. A successful defensive back perfects the important skills of the position and then molds them into one smooth movement. This gives the defensive back the ability to cover even the fastest offensive wide receiver.

When starting to run backward, the defensive back must explode off his front foot. With his front foot under his nose and turned in, he is able to use the muscles in both the outside of his foot and his lower leg to provide this explosion. When pushing off the front foot, he must thrust his hips backward as he steps back with his back foot. As he takes his second step, his shoulders slowly begin to rise.

a   b   c

Figure 9.1 Defensive back stances: *(a)* corner; *(b)* inside strong safety; *(c)* free safety.

This start should be practiced over and over again—pushing off the front foot, thrusting the hips back, stepping back with the back foot, and beginning to run backward in an easy fluid motion.

Backpedaling

One of the most important skills for any defensive back to master is running backward. After the defensive back is comfortable getting into the stance and getting a good start, he is ready to continue his backward movement away from the line of scrimmage.

The speed and quickness of a good defensive back running backward or backpedaling into coverage is amazing. Many of the top cornerbacks can run backward for 10 or 15 yards almost as fast as a receiver can run forward.

Once he has pushed back in his start and stepped with his back foot, the defensive back is in position to continue backpedaling. He accomplishes this by lifting his feet and actually stepping back with each stride he takes. It is important for the defensive back to maintain good body position and movement as he runs backward. His hips remain over his feet, and he maintains a slight forward lean at the waist, keeping his shoulders in front of his hips. He reaches back with each step, hitting on the balls of his feet. His feet are no wider than his hips. He moves his arms in a normal running motion. He keeps his head up. The backpedal looks relaxed, smooth, and continuous. In man coverage, the defensive back focuses on the receiver. In zone coverage, he focuses on the quarterback.

The backward movement should be a true run. Some defensive backs lean so far back that their hips, shoulders, and head are actually behind the feet. A defensive back making this mistake will feel like he is pushing himself backward rather than running backward, landing on his heels instead of the balls of his feet. When this happens, the defensive back should stop backpedaling, go back, and start again. To correctly run backward, he must keep his hips over his feet and his shoulders and head in front of his hips.

Angle Backpedaling

Next, the defensive back must learn to adjust his backward run from a straight line to an angle. One of the goals of any good wide receiver is to adjust his pass route to force the defensive back to turn and leave his backward run. When the defensive back is running toward his own goal line, the receiver has a much better chance to separate from the defensive back on any short or medium pass route.

Learning to stay in the backward run requires practice, but once mastered, it improves coverage. This technique requires the defensive back to change the direction of his backward run without crossing his feet or turning his shoulders. After backpedaling straight for 5 yards, the defensive back angles to his left by swinging his right leg around to change direction. As his right leg swings around, his hips and shoulders remain square and in the proper position for the backpedal. To return to a straight backpedal, he swings his left leg around to change direction. To angle backpedal to the right, he changes the direction of his backpedal by swinging his left leg back and around.

The distance between the defensive back's feet should be less than the width of his hips, and he should move back with each step, landing on the balls of his feet. His hips should stay over his feet, and he should have a slight forward bend at the waist so that his shoulders and head are in front of his hips and feet. The movement should be smooth. His arms should pump easily as he runs.

The four fundamental defensive back techniques are stance, start, backward run, and angle backward run. To be successful as a defensive back, a player must perfect each technique.

Rolling Over

Great wide receivers never lose their momentum when they go into their pattern and change direction. If anything, they get faster as they run their route. If the receiver maintains his speed, it is vital for the defensive back to keep going at full speed. The key to keeping up momentum is to always roll over the foot in the direction the defensive back desires to go. Learning this skill plus knowing exactly the path to take to get to the interception point makes a much better defensive back.

To get an idea of what it feels like to roll over, the player should stand on the sideline, facing the field. He keeps his feet even and hip-width apart. Without turning his body, he leans his head, shoulders, and upper body to the right. As his body moves over his right foot, he will feel his left leg automatically come across the front of his body, and he will take a step in the direction of his lean. He should repeat the drill leaning and rolling over his left foot.

The defensive back should try the same technique from the backward run. Starting at half speed, the defensive back runs backward for 10 yards. He leaves his backward run and quickly changes to a forward run at a 45-degree angle deep to his left by leaning his upper body back and to the left, rolling over his left foot. As he leans, he turns his shoulders to the left. He will feel his right foot automatically come across the front of his body as he continues on his run.

Rolling over is one of the most basic and important techniques for defensive backs. When they can change from a backward run to a forward run without interrupting their momentum and losing their speed, they have a chance to play in the NFL.

It is important to remember that rolling over does not start with the feet. It starts with leaning the upper body in the direction the defensive back desires to go and then allowing his feet to follow in natural, easy steps. If a player's feet slip out from under him or if he has the receiver covered and then in the next step sees him 2 yards away, often the reason is loss of momentum. This happens when the defensive back plants one foot, stops his momentum, and then starts chasing the receiver again.

MAN-TO-MAN COVERAGE

The defensive back must first play the pass. On every play, it is a good idea for defensive backs to start by moving backward away from the line of scrimmage. If the offense runs the ball, the defensive back can stop and come up to make the tackle. If he comes up first, thinking that the play is a run although it is a pass, the receiver may be so far down the field that the defensive back will not be able recover in time to make the tackle or cause an incompletion. It is important for the defensive back to remember that he is the last line of defense. He must think about the pass first. Then he can get involved in stopping the run.

In man-to-man pass defense, the defensive back looks at the man he is covering; in zone pass defense, he looks at the quarterback. In zone pass defense, the defensive back should see the ball when it leaves the quarterback's hand, but in man-to-man he may not see the ball until the very last instant.

Man-to-man pass defense is one of the most exciting challenges for any defensive back. It is usually only the defensive back against his opponent. In some defenses, he may have help in the middle of the field, but he still knows it is his responsibility to keep the receiver from catching the ball.

Pass Route Zones

A defensive back playing man-to-man pass defense must understand the three sets of offensive pass patterns run at different distances down the field. The short zone starts at the line of scrimmage and covers the first 6 yards down the field. The medium zone begins at 7 yards and continues to 12 yards past the line of scrimmage. The deep zone is from 13 yards to the goal line (see figure 4.15, page 77).

It is important for the defensive back to know and be able to recognize these three zones. During a play, he concentrates only on the pass patterns that can be run in that zone. If he worries about recognizing every pass route a receiver might run at the start of every play, he will quickly become flustered and end up guessing rather than recognizing the pass pattern. When the defensive back knows the zones, he only has to think about and recognize the patterns that can be run in that area.

Instead of thinking about 13 or 14 patterns, he can concentrate on recognizing the 3 or 4 run in that zone.

When playing in pass coverage, the defensive back should always cover on one side of the wide receiver or the other. He should never be directly in front of the receiver.

Pattern Recognition

One of the most important skills for a defensive back to learn is to recognize offensive pass routes (pattern recognition). When learning to recognize offensive pass patterns, it is important for the defensive back to work on recognition and not reacting to the pattern. The first thing to do is learn the names of the pass routes he will face.

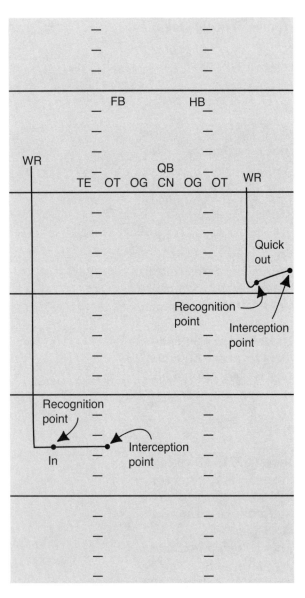

Figure 9.2 Recognition and interception points for a medium pass pattern to the inside of the field and a short pattern to the sideline.

It is best to start with the short pass routes. For wide receivers, the slant, hitch, and quick out patterns are the short pass routes. The tight end's short pass routes are the look-in, short, and flat pass routes. Practicing with a teammate and alternating from offense to defense will help the player to recognize a pattern and run the pattern correctly.

The point at which a defensive back recognizes the pass pattern is called the recognition point. The spot where the ball will be caught is called the interception point. To figure out the interception point, the defensive back must know where the receiver can first catch the ball. On any short or medium pass pattern coming to the inside of the field, the receiver will run at least 6 yards from the recognition point before he can catch the pass (figure 9.2). For a short or medium pattern going toward the sideline, the receiver will cover at least 8 yards from the recognition point before he can make the reception (figure 9.2). The defensive back must concentrate on the receiver as he runs the route in order to recognize the pattern as soon as possible and find the interception point.

After learning to recognize short pass routes, the defensive back must learn the medium pass routes. For the wide receiver, the medium pass routes are the out, in, and hook routes. The tight end's medium patterns are the cross, hook, and out. The medium pass zone covers from 7 yards to 12 yards up the field.

After correctly identifying medium routes, the defensive back can learn the patterns used in the deep pass zone. Once the receiver passes 12 yards, the defensive back should look for the deep pass routes. The wide receiver's deep routes are the post, corner, up, and comeback. The tight end's deep routes are the post, up, and corner. Even on these deep routes, it is important for the defensive back to try to keep 3 yards between himself and the receiver. Deep pass routes to the inside of the field have an interception point of 10 yards (figure 9.3). The interception point for deep patterns to the outside of the field is 12 or more yards (figure 9.3).

The defensive back should focus only on the patterns in the zone. When the receiver passes 6 yards, the defensive back can forget about the pass patterns run in the short zone and concentrate on recognizing the pass patterns run in the medium zone. After the receiver passes 12 yards, the defensive back's focus should be only on deep pass patterns. This thought process is very important. It helps the defensive back relax during his backward run and look only for the patterns run in that zone. The patterns to look for change as the receiver comes off the line of scrimmage and runs up the field.

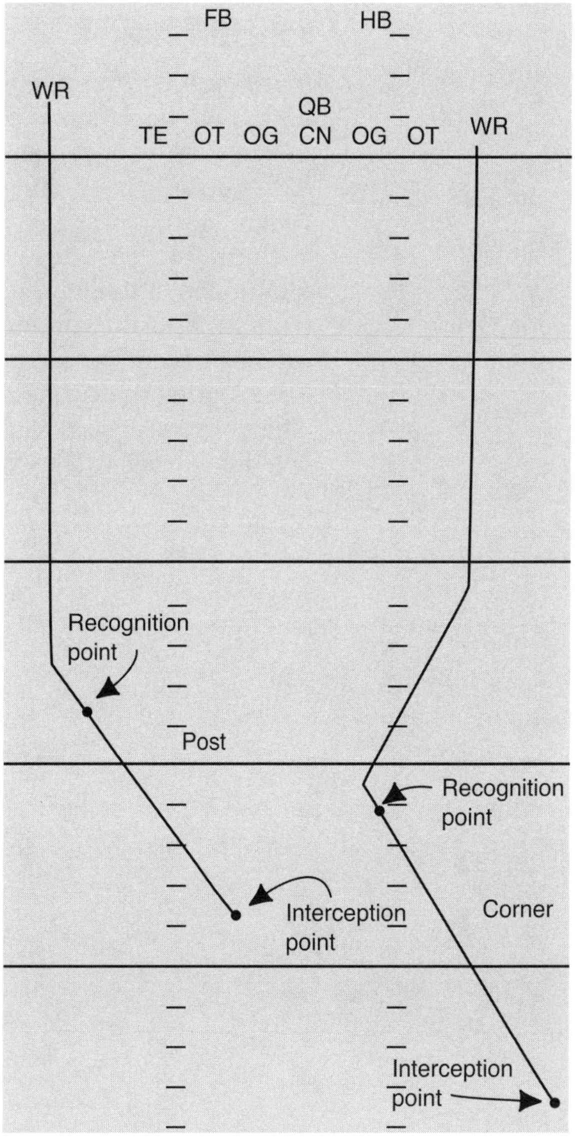

ZONE COVERAGE

For a defensive back, zone coverage is much different than man-to-man. When playing man-to-man coverage, the defensive back covers one offensive receiver all over the field for the entire play. The focus is on that one receiver, and the receiver determines where defensive back should go. The only real chance to look for the ball is when the defensive back is in position to see the receiver and the ball.

Playing zone pass coverage requires the defensive back to change his way of thinking. On the snap of the ball, the defensive back moves to a predetermined area of the field. His focus is on the quarterback, not on a particular receiver. The direction of the pass tells him where to go (ball reaction) instead of a receiver's pass pattern.

The defensive back can and should use all the techniques for man-to-man coverage in zone pass defense. He can backpedal into his zone and angle backpedal if necessary to stay in the proper position on the field.

Figure 9.3 Recognition and interception points for deep pass routes to the inside and to the outside.

Once the ball leaves the quarterback's hand, he should roll over to leave his backpedal. There are no new techniques, but the defensive back must change his focus to the quarterback. He must not allow himself to get distracted by receivers running across the zone.

Zone defenses can be broken down into three types of zone pass coverages. There is a two-deep zone, a three-deep zone, and sometimes a four-deep zone (used against wide open passing teams). In all three zone defenses, the number-one rule is that if the defensive back is covering a deep zone, he must backpedal deep enough to stay between his goal line and the deepest offensive receiver in his zone.

Before the play begins, the defensive back must know which type of pass coverage has been called, zone or man-to-man. If zone pass coverage is called, he needs to know where to go, which zone to cover, how he is going to get to his zone, and what his responsibilities are once he reaches his zone.

Two-Deep Zone

In a two-deep zone (figure 9.4), usually both safeties drop deep. Each safety covers half of the field. It is important for the safeties to backpedal as quickly as possible, get as deep as possible, stay deeper than any receiver in their half of the field, look at the quarterback, and react the instant the quarterback steps and throws the ball (get a jump).

Both corners, who cover the outside underneath zones with the linebackers, should leave their original alignment before the play begins and move to 5 yards from the line of scrimmage. After the snap, the corners take position just outside the offensive receivers as they move up the field. They bump the receivers to the inside, interrupting their runs up the field and forcing the receivers in toward the safeties. The corners drop back to 12 yards using their backpedal technique and focus on the quarterback. They react when the ball leaves the quarterback's hand.

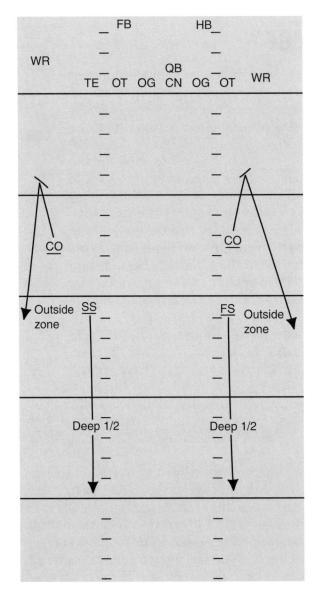

Figure 9.4 Two-deep zone.

Three-Deep Zone

In a three-deep zone (figure 9.5), three of the four defensive backs drop into a deep zone. One of the defensive backs, usually the strong safety, moves up and to the outside to cover the under zone on his side of the field.

Instead of only two defensive backs covering deep, there now are three. Each defensive back, usually the two corners and the free safety, is responsible for covering one-third of the field, or they may have one-quarter, one-quarter, and half coverage. The two corners have the outside third of the field on their side and the free safety moves to cover the center of the field. With three defensive backs going deep, it will be much harder for the offense to complete a pass in the deep zone.

It is important for the defensive back to backpedal as quickly as he can, get as deep as he can, stay deeper than any receiver in his half of the field, look at the quarterback, and react the instant the quarterback steps and throws the ball.

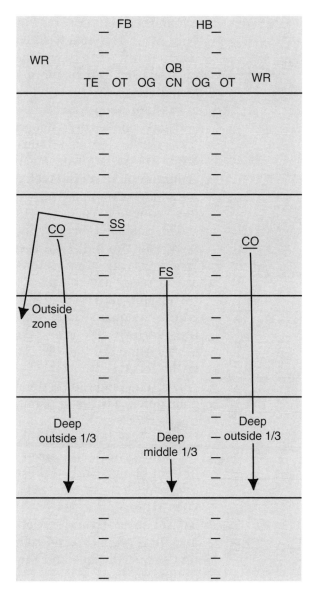

Figure 9.5 Three-deep zone.

The safety who does not have deep coverage uses a different technique to drop into his zone. The technique he uses depends on how wide from his original position he has to go to get into his zone. The wider he has to go, the more he will have to sprint to get there. When he sprints, he rolls over the foot in the direction he needs to go and runs as fast as he can to his area. He constantly looks back over his shoulder to the quarterback. Once he reaches his zone, he swings his inside leg around and gets into his backpedal. As he starts his backpedal, he focuses on the quarterback. He stops his backpedal when he sees that the quarterback is ready to throw. He runs in place, keeping his feet moving in short, choppy steps. He must be prepared to move to either his right or left once he sees the quarterback start the throwing motion. He breaks to the ball by rolling over the foot in the direction he needs to go.

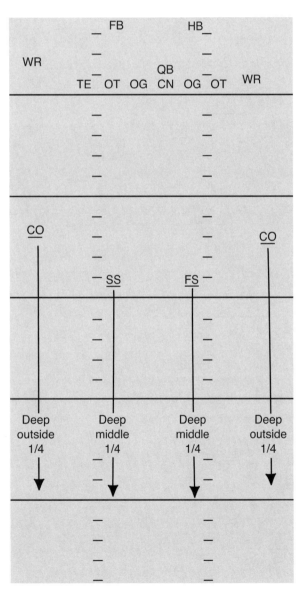

Figure 9.6 Four-deep zone.

Four-Deep Zone

A four-deep zone coverage probably will be used only when the coach knows that the offense has to throw deep to win the game or when the offense uses four or more wide receivers in a formation.

In a four-deep zone (figure 9.6), both corners and both safeties drop deep and cover one-quarter of the field. Any ball thrown deep should be either knocked down, causing an incompletion, or intercepted. All the techniques for defensive backs covering in a deep zone apply in a four-deep zone defense.

The defensive backs should let the quarterback and the ball take them to the receiver. When playing zone defense, the main rules are to recognize the pass, go immediately to the appropriate zone, get as deep as possible before the quarterback sets to throw, focus on the quarterback and the ball, and react to the pass, letting the ball direct the defensive back to the receiver.

One challenge for a defensive back playing zone defense is the urge to take his eyes off the quarterback and look at a receiver running in his zone. Another is the urge to come up before the ball is thrown to cover a receiver running in front of him. Both of these challenges can be overcome if the defensive back practices alone, goes to his zone, looks to where the quarterback will set up, stops and settles into his backpedal, and then reacts to the right or left. Focusing on the quarterback and the ball also gives the defensive back a great chance to make the interception.

PLAYING THE RUN

A defensive back's first concern is to play pass defense. His second is to know what to do when the offense runs the ball. His action and technique are determined by the defense the coach calls for the play. The defensive back must understand his responsibility for the defense called, know what the offense must do before he leaves his pass coverage to attack the line of scrimmage (run force), know where and what his responsibilities are when he forces the run, understand which offensive players can block him, and know how to meet the blocker.

When the defense is called, the defensive back knows he will play either zone or man-to-man pass defense. If the defensive back is responsible for covering a deep zone, he must go to that zone until the ball carrier crosses the line of scrimmage. If he is to cover a receiver man-to-man, he needs to run with his receiver until the receiver blocks or the ball carrier crosses the line of scrimmage. In either case, the defensive back pursues the ball carrier after he is certain that the ball cannot be passed.

A defensive back playing zone defense but not assigned to a deep zone needs to leave his zone and come to the line of scrimmage if the end man on the defensive back's side blocks. If the player he is covering man-to-man blocks immediately, like a tight end on a linebacker, the defensive back may have to come up and help stop the run. The defensive back must not look at the running back or he will be fooled if the running back fakes the run on a pass play. Who is blocking and how they block will give the defensive back a better idea if the offense is running or passing the ball.

When coming up to force the run, the defensive back usually is the outside man of the defense. His job is to quickly force the ball carrier back to the inside of the field. It is important to force the ball carrier back to the inside because all the other defensive players will be pursuing from that direction. The defensive back should not allow the ball carrier to go around him and get to the outside. The defensive back should set a predetermined spot for the force 2 yards in the offensive backfield and 3 yards outside his next defensive teammate. If he can reach this spot, he can force the ball carrier back to the inside and not give the ball carrier a huge running lane up the field.

As he is crossing the line of scrimmage, the defensive back should look for the offensive player who has been assigned to block him. Often this is the fullback, but it can be the offensive tackle or guard. Before the defensive back even thinks about tackling the ball carrier, he must pick out and defeat the offensive blocker.

It is important that the defensive back keep his outside arm and leg free from the blocker. If the ball carrier does try to go around him, the defensive back will be in position to turn to the sideline and make the tackle.

The defensive back should not sit and wait for the blocker to come to him, especially if the blocker is a big offensive lineman. He is far better off if he attacks the blocker, getting his shoulder pads under the offensive man's shoulder pads. He should hit the blocker as hard as he can with his inside forearm. He can bounce back if necessary but he should stay on his feet.

Sometime during every game, the defensive back will be asked to force on a running play. Playing the run is 70 percent desire. The defensive back must be ready and understand how important it is for him to come up the instant he sees that it is a run and not a pass.

DEFENSIVE BACK DRILLS

During every practice defensive backs should go through drills designed to perfect their coverage techniques: start, backpedal, angle backpedal, and rolling over drills. Every practice should include a tackling drill, and at least two catching drills should be run per week (see chapter 1). Conduct the drills at half speed, increasing the tempo as the player's skill improves. The time spent on these daily drills should become less and less once the players master the individual techniques.

Exploding at the Start

Purpose: To teach defensive backs to explode at the start of the play.

Procedure:

1. The coach lines up in front of the defensive back.
2. Once the defensive back is in a proper stance, the coach calls "Hut."
3. The defensive back explodes at the start, moving back.

Variation: To include backpedaling, use the same setup. The coach can stand at the side of the defensive back if he thinks the defensive back is leaning back. To practice the angle backpedal, the coach points in the direction the defensive back should go after backpedaling for 10 yards.

Coaching Points: The player must step back with his back foot and propel his hips away from the line of scrimmage. His head and shoulders should come up gradually and never be behind the feet and hips.

Staying in the Backpedal

Purpose: To reinforce proper backpedal and angle backpedal technique.

Procedure:

1. The defensive back lines up in position. The coach stands in front of the defensive back.
2. On the coach's signal, the defensive back explodes at the start and begins to backpedal.
3. After the defensive back runs 5 yards straight back, the coach signals the defensive back to angle to the left.
4. After 5 yards running on the angle, the coach signals the defensive back to return to the straight backpedal.
5. After 5 yards of the straight backpedal, the coach signals the defensive back to angle to the right. The defensive back runs the right angle for 5 yards.

Variation: After the player can do the drill for 20 yards, he can roll over in the direction the coach indicates rather than angling in that direction, going from a backpedal to a forward run.

Coaching Points: The defensive back maintains the backward run throughout the drill. It is important to maintain proper body position during the entire 20 yards. He must never cross his feet during the angle drill. The player must change direction for a rollover by leaning his body in the direction indicated, rolling over the foot on that side, and turning into a forward run.

Pass Zones

Purpose: To teach defensive backs the passing zones.

Procedure:

1. The coach lines up to the side of the defensive back. Another defensive back, acting as a wide receiver, lines up.
2. The defensive back lines up 9 yards away from the wide receiver.
3. The coach calls the snap count to start the play.
4. The wide receiver jogs up the field. The defensive back backpedals for 20 yards.
5. When the wide receiver enters the short zone, the defensive back calls out, "Short, short, short." When the wide receiver passes 6 yards, the defensive back calls out, "Medium, medium, medium." Finally after 12 yards, the defensive back calls out, "Deep, deep, deep."

Coaching Points: When practicing with a teammate, the defensive back can start 9 or 10 yards away from the receiver, allowing him to stay in his backward run the entire time the receiver runs up the field 20 yards. He is practicing recognizing the different pass zones, not working on the backward run. The receiver should run at half speed at first, increasing his speed as the defensive back correctly calls out the distance for each zone.

During this drill, the defensive back lines up on one side of the receiver and stays on that side as the receiver runs up the field. The defensive back should always cover on one side or the other and never end up directly in front of the receiver.

Recognizing Pass Patterns

Purpose: To give defensive backs experience recognizing pass patterns.

Procedure:

1. The coach lines up behind a defensive back acting as a wide receiver. The defensive back lines up in his normal position and stance.
2. The coach tells the wide receiver which route to run-short, medium, or deep.
3. The coach calls out the snap and the receiver runs the route.
4. As the receiver starts off the line, the defensive back goes into his backward run.
5. The moment he recognizes the pattern (recognition point), the defensive back calls out the name of the pattern and points to where the receiver will catch the ball (interception point). He keeps moving backward as he does so.

Variation: Once the player can correctly call and point out all the pass routes in the three different zones, the coach can run with the drill and have the defensive back break to the interception point for each pass route.

Coaching Points: Work on one zone at a time. Only after the defensive back correctly calls and points out each pattern run in each zone without a mistake should the receiver and the defensive back run patterns in another zone. Do not use a ball when teaching man-to-man pass technique. Force the defensive back to concentrate on the receiver and react to his pass route.

Playing a Two-Deep Zone

Purpose: To give the defensive backs experience playing a two-deep zone.

Procedure:

1. The coach lines up in the quarterback position with a ball. Four defensive backs line up in their normal positions.
2. The coach calls out which defensive backs are to drop back and snaps the ball to start the drill.
3. Defensive backs drop back into their coverage. The coach should raise the ball to indicate the pass is about to be thrown.

Variations: This drill is also good for practicing three-deep and four-deep zones. To give the defensive backs practice following the ball to the receiver, actually throw the ball. The defensive backs move to the ball.

Coaching Points: Players covering a deep zone should work hard to get as deep as possible as quickly as they can. Any defensive back in an under zone should move quickly to his zone and then backpedal to get his depth until the coach raises the ball to throw. As he steps toward a target area, all four defensive backs should move in that direction. Teach zone coverage using a ball and not a receiver.

Pass or Run

Purpose: To help the defensive back understand his responsibility for the called defense.

Procedure:

1. The coach lines up facing the defensive back and even with the fullback. Another defensive back lines up as a tight end and another lines up as a linebacker in front of the tight end.
2. The coach calls out coverage and the offensive play, sweep or pass.
3. If sweep, the tight end blocks and the fullback becomes a blocker on the defensive back.
4. If pass, the tight end releases up the field and the fullback sets up to pass protect.
5. The defensive back comes up or drops back based on the play.

Coaching Points: Based on the coverage called by the coach, the designated defensive back who does not have deep zone coverage (corner or safety) must key the tight end and react accordingly. He should locate his force spot, 2 yards across the line of scrimmage and 3 yards outside of the linebacker, and head there the moment the tight end blocks. If the tight end releases upfield, the defensive back reacts according to the coverage called. He should take on any blocker with his inside shoulder and keep his outside leg and arm free when coming up on any running play.

Special Teams

Special teams involve a lot of players and many different skills. This chapter covers punts, field goals, kickoffs, and kick returns. Special teams play includes the placekicker, short snapper, and holder, who must work as one unit; the two-unit team of the punter and the long snapper; kickoff and punt returners.

KICKERS

Punter and placekicker are two of the most responsible positions on the team. Other players have the luxury of knowing that if they mess up on a play they will have many more opportunities during the game to do it right. A punter or placekicker may have only a few opportunities during a game, and the pressure is on to get it right every time.

The most important attribute for a kicker is the ability to focus on the upcoming kick. He must be able to concentrate on making one kick at a time. Great kickers and punters work hard to be the best-conditioned athletes on the football team and to have a mental toughness that allows them to focus completely on the job at hand. Whether punting out of his own end zone or lining up for a last-second, game-winning field goal, the kicker's attitude is, "Give me the chance. Let's get out on the field, and I will get the job done."

Every kicker experiences problems when he starts out. Beginning kickers must work hard, focus, stay positive, and try to improve with every kick they make. This chapter covers the techniques for punting and placekicking, the stance and steps, the drop when punting, the plant foot when placekicking, and the mental and physical skills a successful kicker needs.

The kicker's beginning stance must be functional and help him perform the physical movements of punting or placekicking. A good stance can improve performance and is essential to becoming a great punter or placekicker.

A good start is crucial for both the punter and the placekicker. Their initial steps greatly influence the outcome of the kick. Each kicker must have a set, practiced start in his kicking motion. A true beginner should start learning the steps by walking through them, slowly increasing his forward movement as he becomes comfortable with the action.

When the kicker is first learning technique, he shouldn't use the ball. It is human nature to want to kick the ball immediately, but once the ball is introduced it becomes the center of attention. All the hard work on stance, steps, and kicking can quickly be forgotten if kicking the ball assumes major importance. The more techniques the kicker masters before using the ball, the greater his opportunity for success. The kicker should focus first on getting the techniques down and making them automatic. This makes kicking the ball much easier.

After a punter or placekicker has practiced getting into a comfortable stance and feels that he has established the correct steps, the next technique to work on is his kicking. He must establish a fluid kicking motion. Both placekickers and punters should practice their kicking motions over and over again without using a ball. Every phase is important. They must use a proper stance, use the correct steps, and develop a fluid kicking motion.

Once they've mastered the basic techniques, it is time to introduce the ball into practice. If at any time the player has trouble punting or placekicking, the player should practice without the ball.

THREE-UNIT TEAM: PLACEKICKER, SHORT SNAPPER, AND HOLDER

Success is a team effort. To have a successful kick, the kicker and his teammates must do their jobs. The blockers must keep the defensive players from blocking the kick. The center must make the snap. The holder must catch the snap and place the ball on the spot. The kicker must concentrate and kick the ball correctly.

For a placekicker to be successful, two other players must do their jobs correctly. The placekicker should understand the role of the short snapper and holder, because any field goal or extra point is a joint effort. Improper technique by any of the three can result in the failure of the kick.

Placekicker

The placekicker is in a unique position. Every time he goes out on the field, he has the opportunity to score points. No other player has this opportunity, but with this opportunity comes tremendous responsibility.

The placekicker's stance should be comfortable (figure 10.1a). The placekicker gets into his stance the same way every time. First he stands straight up and steps forward with his nonkicking (plant) foot. The heel of the plant foot is just ahead of the toe of his kicking foot. His feet are no wider than his hips and his weight is distributed evenly on both feet. He slightly bends both knees and bends forward at the waist, moving his shoulders forward so that they are in front of his hips. He relaxes his shoulders and allows his hands and arms to hang comfortably. He focuses on the kicking tee.

When the player is in a comfortable stance, he is ready to start moving to make the kick. The initial movement forward toward the placement spot starts with a slight forward lean of his shoulders. Then he takes a short momentum step forward with his plant foot, a normal forward step with his kicking foot (figure 10.1b), and a longer step with his plant foot. The step with his plant foot should bring the kicker's foot even with and six inches outside of the placement spot (where the holder will place the ball for the kick). In this position, the kicker has room and is in position to make contact with the ball. Soon he will feel that his steps are the correct length and that he is ending in the proper position to make the kick, with his head down and eyes on the placement spot.

Most placekickers are soccer-style kickers. The power for the kick starts when the hips move forward and the kicking leg comes forward in a full arch. The knee of the kicking leg must precede the foot toward the placement spot (figure 10.1c). The knee of the kicking leg should be bent back slightly. The position of the kicking foot is important. The toes should point down and the kicker's ankle should be locked and stable.

The toe of the kicking foot passes just outside the placement spot. The center of the inside of the kicking foot passes directly over the center of the placement spot. The top inside of the center of the kicking foot is the part of the foot that makes contact with the ball (figure 10.1d).

The follow-through (figure 10.1e) is an excellent indication of how the kick will go. When the kicking foot moves over the placement spot, the entire body must move straight at the target. As his kicking foot moves over the placement spot, the

a

b

Figure 10.1 Placekicker's motion: *(a)* initial stance; *(b)* steps to the ball; *(c)* swings the kicking leg; *(d)* makes contact with the ball; *(e)* follows through.

c

d

e

175

kicker's body is balanced, his head is down, and his eyes are focused on the placement spot. His hips lead the way to the target. Throughout the kicking motion, the kicker's shoulders precede his feet. A coach or teammate can line up 4 or 5 yards in front of the placement spot to watch the kicker's motion, making certain the kicker follows through by moving straight toward him.

Before the kicker can get into his kicking motion with a ball, he must learn to align himself properly to the placement spot. When practicing by himself, the kicker can place a kicking tee, a cup, or a piece of tape on the ground to indicate the placement spot. Once he establishes this spot, he needs to step correctly to get into proper position to start the kick. To line up to make the kick, the kicker places his plant foot so the instep of the foot is next to the placement spot, and he places his kicking foot directly behind the placement spot. Beginning with his kicking foot, he takes three normal steps straight back from the placement spot and then two steps at a right angle with his plant foot. He turns and faces the placement spot and gets into his stance.

When first learning to kick, the kicker may find that he is not stepping straight back from the placement spot. One way to correct this is to put the placement spot on a marked sideline on the field. Then he can see if he has stepped straight down the line. When moving forward with his steps, the kicker's plant foot should come down even with and six inches outside the placement spot. He points his toe in exactly the same direction as the kicking spot. This foot position is easy to monitor when working on the sideline.

Each time the kicker practices a kick, he should establish a placement spot. He needs to take the time to follow the exact steps to get lined up properly. Once he is in position, he assumes a comfortable stance. When ready, he takes the correct steps to the placement spot and makes sure that his plant foot comes down in the right position. He executes his kicking motion in a smooth manner and makes certain that his body follows through directly at the target.

The kicker needs to be alert to whether his follow-through goes off to the left or the right instead of straight to the target. If he is going off to the left, he should make sure his shoulders are not behind his hips. Going off to the right is caused by the kicker misplacing his plant foot or putting his shoulders too far in front of his feet.

Once the entire kicking motion has become automatic and the kicker feels comfortable with every phase of the kick, it is time to introduce the ball. Eliminating the goalpost and focusing solely on kicking the ball in a straight line will help the kicker concentrate on technique. To kick without a goalpost, the kicker should practice on a sideline, making the placement spot a point where a yard line meets the sideline. The kicker takes his steps and sets up. A coach or a fellow kicker places the ball on the placement spot, making certain the laces of the ball point straight down the sideline. The kicker finishes by kicking the ball in a straight line directly down the sideline. He should make sure he performs each technique correctly.

To stay smooth and accurate, the kicker's goal is to kick with a natural motion. Because the kicker is focusing on accuracy, there is no need for a center. The kicker should be careful to not overkick (kick too hard) now that he is practicing with the ball.

Accuracy, not distance, is the goal. By kicking the ball down the sideline, the kicker will be able to quickly tell if he is hooking or pushing the ball as he kicks. If he finds that he cannot get the ball to travel straight down the sideline, he needs to take the ball out of the drill and review each part of his kicking motion with the coach.

Once the season rolls around, a kicker's participation in practice time may be limited, especially if he does not play another position. Still, he needs to keep busy during the season. He must work on his conditioning every day. He should develop a daily stretching program to improve flexibility, a daily running program that includes sprints and distance running, and a program to increase the strength of his abdominal muscles. It is the kicker's responsibility to work as hard as his teammates during practice and to always be in the best condition he can be. This not only benefits the kicker, it also makes him feel more a part of the team.

The player and the coach should set the exact number of kicks the kicker will make each day, and the kicker should stay within that number. His concentration should be on making kicks correctly, focusing on the proper techniques for each kick.

Short Snapper

The ball originates with the center. The center needs to position his body to make the snap to the holder, who is 7 yards away. The center makes the snap primarily with one hand. The other hand is on the ball, but only as a guide.

The center must think of the snap to the holder as a pass thrown back between his legs. In order to get this passing motion, he must make certain the ball is in front of him when he gets into his stance (figure 10.2a). The center wants a comfortable, balanced stance. His feet should be at least shoulder-width apart and even. If he feels more comfortable, the foot on the side of his snapping hand can be slightly behind his other foot. His shoulders should be square to the line of scrimmage and his hips and shoulders should be even. The center's hips control the height of his snap—high hips, high snap; low hips, low snap.

a   b

Figure 10.2   Short snapper's *(a)* stance and *(b)* grip.

Once in this position, the center reaches out for the ball. He should be sure to rotate the laces of the ball to the outside and down so that they are just past the center point. The center should grip the ball just as if he were a quarterback throwing a forward pass. A proper grip ensures the desired accuracy and velocity.

The size of the player's hands in relationship to the ball will determine the way he is able to grasp the football. Regardless of the size of his snapping hand, he starts by gripping the ball near the center (figure 10.2b). He places three fingers of his snapping hand on or over the laces of the ball. The index finger is near the tip of the ball off the laces and across the seam of the ball where the laces are. The middle and third finger are across the laces. The fingertips of these two fingers are on the surface of the ball, not on the laces. The little finger just reaches the laces of the ball. He feels most of the pressure between the ball and the passing hand just in front of the center point on the front of the ball.

At this point, the center places his other hand lightly on the top of the ball and he prepares to snap. He looks back through his legs to the holder. The holder's hands are always the center's target. When the holder has both hands extended and is ready to catch the ball, the center knows he can snap the ball back to the holder.

As he snaps the ball back between his legs, the center makes certain to follow through with both hands. The fingers of both hands should point directly at the holder's hands. In a really good follow-through, he will feel his entire body move slightly back toward the holder and kicker as he makes the snap.

Holder

The holder must position himself on the opposite side of the placement spot from the kicker. Once even with the tee, the holder kneels down with his back knee on the ground 7 yards from the center (figure 10.3). The foot of his front leg is up, with his toe pointed directly at the goalpost. From this position, he leans slightly forward toward the center.

Figure 10.3 Holder ready for the snap.

The holder places his back hand on the center of the tee and extends his front hand and arm, palm down, toward the center. The holder's front arm and hand form the top part of the center's target. They should be even with the center of the holder's chest. The holder then asks the kicker if he is ready. When the kicker says he is ready, the holder brings his other hand off the ground and forms a target for the center's snap. His thumbs should be touching so he can catch the ball correctly. The center will see that he has extended both hands toward him, and the center will feel free to snap the ball at any time. The holder must be alert!

Obviously, it would be nice if the ball zipped back into the holder's hands at the right spot on every kick. That will not always be the case, and the holder must be prepared to catch the snap no matter where it is. The holder's first job is to make the catch, then get the ball down onto the kicking tee. After making the catch, the holder uses one smooth motion to place the ball on the tee. He turns the ball so that the laces face the goalposts as he brings the ball down. The holder rotates the ball to the correct position with his front hand as he places the tip of the ball on the tee. He places the index finger of his back hand lightly on the top point of the ball to balance it at the correct position for the kicker (figure 10.4).

Figure 10.4 Holder ready for the kick.

Everyone must do his job to create a successful kick. Once the center completes the snap, the holder makes the catch and places the ball on the placement spot, and the blockers stop the rushers, it all comes down to executing the kick. The kicker must concentrate on the placement spot, stay smooth during his approach, maintain his technique, be fluid in his kicking motion, keep his head down, use a good follow-through, and listen for the crowd to tell him that it is good. Make kicking a year-round priority. It is most productive if the kicker, short snapper, and holder work together all through the year. Spring and summer workouts are a great time to focus on each of their separate skills without the pressure of the game.

TWO-UNIT TEAM: PUNTER AND LONG SNAPPER

Every punt can affect the outcome of the game. A successful punt requires the work of all 11 players on the field. The blockers must keep the defensive players from blocking the kick, the center must make the long snap back to the punter, and the punter must catch the ball and execute the punt. Everyone must cover the kick to tackle the return man before he can gain yardage. Everyone must do his job, but the center and the punter are responsible for kicking the punt and must work in unison as a smooth two-man team.

Punter

The team's punter is in a unique position. He has the opportunity to cause a great change in field position with every punt. With a good punt and good coverage, he has the opportunity to pin the opposition deep in their end of the field.

In any game, there will come a time when the offense is having trouble moving the ball. The punter's kick moves the ball away from his goal line, giving the defense an opportunity to go in and stop the opponent and, at the same time, giving the offense a chance to regroup.

The punter's stance must allow him to move forward to punt the ball. His stance must also put him in position to move to the right or left, bend to the ground, or leap high into the air to catch a poorly snapped ball. To get into his stance, the punter stands straight up with his feet even. He spreads his feet about hip-width apart or slightly wider. He takes a slight step forward with his punting foot so that the toe of his back foot is even with the middle of his kicking foot (figure 10.5). He feels his weight on the balls of both feet. He bends his knees a little and brings his shoulders forward so they are slightly in front of his hips. His head is up with his eyes looking straight ahead.

From this position, the punter should practice moving in every direction without the ball. He must feel comfortable going after any snapped ball no matter where it is, including one sailing over his head. If the punter practices these movements without the ball and without a rush, he will be ready to perform when they occur in practice or a game.

A punter may use either a two- or three-step punting motion. With either motion, the punter's steps should be smooth and he should not overstride. He should picture himself walking toward the ball, never hurrying or leaning back as he steps. Because there is less risk of a blocked punt with the two-step style, focus on it.

Figure 10.5 Punter's stance.

To begin the two-step punt, the punter should be in a comfortable stance with his kicking foot slightly in front of his back foot. He takes a short step with his front foot slightly to the outside instead of straight ahead, landing on the ball of his kicking foot. Next he takes a normal step. The length of this step is the same as if he were walking. This step lands slightly across the center of his body. The punter wants to land on the ball of his foot so he can transfer power to the actual kick.

Maintaining balance and control of the body while moving forward are essential to good punting. One way to maintain position is for the punter to practice the steps with his hands on his hips. In this position, the feet do the work and it is quickly evident if the player is losing his balance. He is now ready to practice positioning the hands and arms to receive the snap. Unlike a placekicker, the punter must learn to receive the snap by himself.

After assuming the proper stance, the punter extends the hand and arm on the same side as his kicking foot directly out in front of his shoulder. He moves the arm so the hand is near the center of his body. He then turns the hand over so the palm faces the ground. This position gives the center the top part of the target. Next, the punter reaches out with the other hand and arm to a level even with the middle of the punter's belly. The palm of this hand faces up. This arm and hand form the bottom half of the center's target.

When the punter is ready and the center has seen the target, the punter moves his top hand down until it is even with his bottom hand. At this point, the palms of both hands face up and the little fingers almost touch (figure 10.6).

In order for the punter to see both his hands and the ball when the ball is snapped, he extends his arms away from his body. At first the punter should practice without the ball (figure 10.7). He starts his normal steps. Both hands remain in position during his first step. When beginning his second step, the punter drops the hand away from his kicking foot. This hand swings back behind his hip. At the same time, he pushes forward the hand on the same side as the kicking foot. This hand should be slightly outside the thigh of the kicking leg. The punter allows the extended hand to drop naturally to his side as the kicking leg comes through in a practice kicking motion.

The fun of kicking, of course, is seeing the ball go where the punter wants it to go. Even NFL kickers know that beginning kickers need to practice the motion of the kick over and over before bringing the ball out on the field. Eventually, though, the punter has to punt the ball. He has the additional task of catching the ball from the center, adjusting it in a proper grip, extending it correctly, and dropping it accurately to his punting foot. The punter should work on the handling of the ball and the drop before working with the center.

The first thing is to make certain the punter grips the ball correctly. The grip starts with the laces facing straight up. The placement of the ball into the hand on the same side as the kicking leg is most important. The back tip of the ball should touch the palm of the hand. The front tip should be midway between the thumb

Figure 10.6 Punter is ready for the snap.

Figure 10.7 At first, the punter should practice the kicking motion without the ball.

Figure 10.8 Punter's grip of the ball.

and forefinger. The thumb should be on the inside top panel of the ball. The forefinger and second finger should be on the outside top panel of the football. The remaining two fingers—the ring and little finger—should be on the outside bottom panel of the ball. The pressure from the thumbs and fingers of the drop hand should allow the punter to hold the ball comfortably and securely (figure 10.8).

The other hand should be on the front inside of the ball, four fingers on the inside under panel and the thumb on the top inside panel just above the side seam. The punter should grasp the ball with as little pressure as necessary. Holding the ball with too much pressure adversely affects the way the punter drops the ball onto his foot.

Now that the punter is holding the ball properly in both hands, he is ready to proceed with the hand, arm, and drop action of the kick. When learning these techniques, it is best if he does not actually kick the ball. This allows the punter to go through these movements a number of times in a very short period. He also does not step while learning the kick.

The actual kicking movement starts when the punter moves his hand away from his kicking foot. The punter allows his hand and arm to swing back to the outside at waist-height, providing balance for the kick. As the hand swings back, the punter's hips turn slightly to the inside in the direction of his arm swing and his opposite shoulder rotates slightly forward. This allows his ball hand and arm to extend easily in front of his body (figure 10.9a).

As he extends the ball, the hand on the side of the punter's kicking foot, his drop hand, rotates the point of the ball slightly to the inside until the ball is aimed in the same direction as the punter's hips. The punter is steady at the wrist and keeps the ball level, not pointing up or down, just above his waist. When the ball is slightly outside the thigh of the kicking leg, he pulls the drop hand away and allows the ball to drop to the ground (figure 10.9b).

During practice when the punter is not actually kicking the ball, if the ball has been dropped correctly it should hit the ground and bounce straight back to his kicking leg. He will know exactly where the ball is going if he focuses on it, as he should during an actual kick. The direction the ball takes after it hits the ground tells the punter if something was wrong with the drop so he can correct the error. If the ball bounces back to the punter but not straight back to his kicking leg, it means that the front point of the ball was the first part to strike the ground. If the ball bounces forward and away from his kicking leg, the back of the ball struck the ground first. The punter should repeat this drill until the ball bounces back to his kicking leg every time he drops it to the ground. He should follow each step, noting the amount of pressure he uses to grip the ball. He should keep the wrist of his drop hand locked as he extends the ball forward in preparation for release.

When the ball is first introduced, the concern is not hang time or distance. The concern is the correct steps, a smooth movement to the point of the kick, a good drop, and an easy leg motion in the kick. Power, distance, and hang time will come once the punter masters the fundamentals of the kick.

When first learning the kicking motion, the punter can start on the sideline. The punter positions himself and holds the ball waist-high in both hands in front of the center of his body. He begins by stepping forward with his kicking foot. During this

a
b

Figure 10.9 Drop action: *(a)* ball hand and arm extend; *(b)* the ball drops.

step, he keeps the ball secure in both hands. The punter makes certain that the length of this step allows him to land on the ball of his kicking foot. He then takes a step with his nonkicking foot. He moves his hand away from the ball as he takes this step. This hand and arm swing back and outside his hip in a smooth motion. The hand with the ball extends forward and slightly outside of the kicking leg as the nonkicking foot hits the ground. The punter is now in position to drop the ball to his kicking foot as his kicking leg comes through in a smooth, coordinated motion (figure 10.10).

For the drop to be successful the punter must be sure to rotate the ball slightly to the inside until it points in the same direction as the punter's hips. The ball must be level, with the point not aiming up or down. The ball should be just above the waist. The punter needs to focus and concentrate on the ball all the way from his drop hand to his kicking foot.

Up to this point, the punter has worked independently on the different segments of the punting action. This is the first time he will attempt to put them all together. In the beginning, the punter may look jerky moving through the kick. This is natural and will improve very quickly. The important thing is for the punter to stay positive.

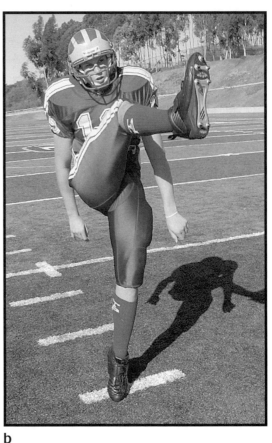

a   b

Figure 10.10 Kicking action: *(a)* punter drops the ball to kicking foot; *(b)* kicking foot comes through in a smooth motion.

A common mistake is for the punter to take a longer first or second step, landing on the heel rather than the ball of the foot. This stops the punter's forward momentum and prevents him from moving smoothly through the entire kicking motion. To prevent or correct this problem, the punter needs to watch the length of his stride.

Another mistake beginning punters often make is forgetting to keep the shoulders and head in front of the hips. This causes the punter to lean back, putting him out of position to drop the ball properly to his kicking foot. Leaning back also can cause the punter to come down on the heel of his foot, even if his stride is the proper length. The punter must focus on keeping the upper body in front of the hips.

When something is wrong, the punter should go back, eliminating the ball and practicing the fundamentals. If one particular aspect is not working, the punter should work on that segment of the kick all by itself without the ball until he is doing it properly. Practicing punting the ball when part of the punt is wrong only reinforces bad habits. The punter must understand what makes a punt successful, what makes a punt bad, and which part of the kicking motion he needs to review to ensure a successful punt.

It may be necessary during the game to punt to the right or left rather than straight down the field. The punter may need to kick away from a very good return man or try to keep his coverage area to one side of the field. The punter's goal when using a directional kick might be to kick the ball out of bounds to pin the opponent deep in his own end of the field.

Good directional punting starts before the punter ever gets the snap from the center. The key is adjusting the placement of the foot opposite the kicking foot. This foot needs to be turned to point in the direction that the punter desires to kick slightly before the punter receives the snap. A right-footed punter adjusts his left foot; a left-footed punter adjusts his right foot.

When a right-footed punter kicks to the left, he turns his left foot to the left so the toe of his left foot points directly where he wants to kick the ball (figure 10.11). If the left foot is not turned, the punter will step across his body with his right foot, disrupting his natural punting motion. By turning the foot before the snap, his first step will be natural with his hips and shoulders square and pointed directly where he wants the ball to go.

Kicking to the right for a right-footed kicker requires a similar adjustment with the left foot. This time he turns his left foot to the right with the toe pointed to where he wants to kick the ball. A right-footed punter tends to step to the right in his natural punting motion. Because of this, he does not have to turn the left foot as much as he does when punting to the left. A slight turn of the left foot to the right keeps his hips and shoulders square and pointed right where he wants the punt to go.

Figure 10.11 Right-footed punter turns his left foot to the left to direct the punt to the left.

Long Snapper

One of the most important positions in punting is the center. Teams usually punt 7 to 10 times a game, and every snap the center makes must be perfect. The center and the punter must work as one unit.

For a punter to be successful, he must have faith that the center is going to deliver the ball into his hands so that he can concentrate on his movement and making the kick. When the punter worries about where the snap is going to go, he doesn't concentrate on the catch, steps, drop, and kick.

The long snap is similar to the short snap in placekicking. Because there are many similarities, it's a good idea to review the stance and grip of the ball covered in the short snapper section of placekicking (see pages 177-178). There are two major differences between the snap for a placekick and the snap for a punt. First, the distance of the snap for a placekick is 7 yards; for a punt, it's 15 yards. Second, the actual height of the snap differs. The short snap for a placekick goes to a holder who is on his knees waiting for the ball. The numbers of the punter's jersey as he stands and waits for the snap are the target area for a long snap on a punt.

Because of the increased distance and the higher target, the center needs to make two changes to his snap. First, he needs to lift the front point of the ball off the ground. Second, he must increase the velocity of the snap.

Before centering the ball, the center needs to establish the target area for the snap. The center looks at the punter's hands for the target. When he sees the punter adjust his hands, turning both palms up, the center knows the punter is ready to receive the ball. When making the snap (figure 10.12), it is important for the center to follow through with both hands, allowing the palms to rotate out and the hands to follow the path of the ball. If this is done with the proper velocity, the center may find that his entire body moves back toward the punter. This is normal.

Snapping the ball to the punter is the center's first and most important job, but it is not his only job on the punt team. After his release and follow-though, the center

a   b

Figure 10.12 Long snap: *(a)* center looks to target area; *(b)* he snaps the ball and follows through with both hands.

can help block any rushers in his immediate area. After the ball is punted, he can sprint downfield to cover the kick and make or help on the tackle of the opposing return man. Often he will be one of the first players down the field on the punt team covering the kick. If he has the ability to tackle in the open field, he can become a very valuable player.

KICKING OFF

The kicker on kickoffs is in position to force the opponent to start his next offensive series deep in his end of the field. It is important to always try to kick the ball high and far. This type of kick gives the cover men the chance to run down the field and tackle the return man before he can gain many yards. Kickoff consistency is important.

One of the easiest ways for the kicker to get into a good, comfortable stance is to stand with both feet together and take a normal step forward with the nonkicking foot. Then the kicker brings that foot back about half the distance to his body. He slightly flexes his knees. He positions his shoulders slightly in front of his hips and allows his arms and hands to hang down in a relaxed manner. Once the kicker has assumed his stance a number of times, he will automatically know the distance to take with the half-step.

When beginning to work on the setup, stance, steps, and kicking motion, the kicker should use only a tee as a point of reference. Later the ball can be added to practice. The kicking tee should be placed on a yard line facing the field. This provides a good reference for setting up and a point for the positioning of the kicker's plant foot. Once the kicking tee is in place, the kicker lines up with his kicking foot directly behind the tee and his nonkicking foot to the side of the tee. From this position, he takes one step away from the tee with his kicking foot and then turns around so that he faces away from the tee. He takes eight normal steps away from the ball straight down the yard line, ending up with his kicking foot on the yard line. He turns to face the tee, making sure he is not to the right or left of the yard line. He turns in the direction of his nonkicking foot and takes five normal steps. Then he turns back to face the tee and prepares to get into his stance. He should end up at a 45-degree angle to the kicking tee as he gets into his stance.

Once the kicker is in position and the proper stance, it is time for him to move to the ball. He starts his forward movement by leaning his shoulders forward. As he leans, he takes a short half-step forward with his nonkicking foot. He stays relaxed during his steps for the first 5 yards of his approach. His pace quickens with each step in the final 5 yards as he approaches the tee. The kicker attacks the tee and prepares for the actual kicking motion.

One of the keys to a good kickoff is to correctly place the plant foot at the start of the kicking motion. The plant foot should strike the ground two to four inches behind the kicking tee and six inches to the left of the kicking tee. His foot should point straight down the field in the direction of the kick (figure 10.13). When the plant foot makes contact with the ground, the kicker must keep his head down and focus his eyes on the tee. His shoulders should be in front of his hips.

Figure 10.13 Placement of the plant foot before the kick.

For a kicker who uses a soccer-style motion, the actual kicking motion (figure 10.14) begins with the hips moving forward. The kicking leg moves forward in a high arc. The toe points down and the knee is in front of the foot. The kicker's foot comes through so that the inside of the instep strikes an inch below the center of the ball. The foot should come through with such power that the kicker lifts off the ground and lands two to three feet in front of the tee.

After the kicker is able to move in the correct way, he can start practicing with the ball. When the ball is on the tee, it should be nearly vertical. It is also important for the laces to be in front, lined up facing where the kicker wants the kick to go.

At first, the kicker should not overkick or see how far he can kick the ball. Instead he needs to concentrate on a smooth kicking motion, striking the ball properly, and seeing that the ball goes straight down the yard line. The kicker can work up to attacking the ball and adding distance to the kickoff in practice sessions.

If the kicker experiences problems with any part of the kick, taking the ball out of practice and reviewing each segment is helpful. Kickoffs will be smooth and effective once the kicker has corrected any faulty part of his kick.

a   b

Figure 10.14 Kicking motion for kickoffs: *(a)* back swing of kicking leg; *(b)* kicker is lifted off the ground and eventually lands in front of the tee on the follow-through.

RETURNING KICKS

A kick returner must be dedicated and fearless in his approach to his job. Every return must be important to him. When returning punts or kickoffs, the kick returner must understand that his return can greatly influence the team's field position. He must focus only on the ball and not be concerned with the opposing players who are racing at him. His concentration must be on making the catch. He must completely secure the ball until the whistle blows, ending the return. He must accept that most likely he will be hit by multiple tacklers every time he returns a kick.

While he needs the same attributes and has the same responsibilities for both punts and kickoffs, there are some differences. First, the flight of the ball differs. A punt comes in a spiral while a kickoff travels end-over-end. Also, a punt usually is much higher than a kickoff. In punting the return man may not be able to see the ball the instant it is punted, but he will have a clear view on a kickoff. Opposing coverage men may be right in front of him when he fields a punt, while on a kickoff he usually has time to make the catch and start up the field before the coverage men reach him. When blocking for the return of a punt, blockers try to keep the coverage men from getting down the field, then they block any opposing player in a specific area. For kickoff returns, blockers are assigned specific players for the entire play. The return man does not have to catch every punt. He can allow the punt to be recovered by the opponent and it will still be his team's ball, but on a kickoff he must catch or fall on the ball because a kickoff is a free ball. Finally, smaller players often return punts, while bigger, stronger players return kickoffs.

Kickoffs

Where the return man positions himself to catch a kickoff depends on the ability of the player kicking the ball. It is a good idea for the return man to line up 10 yards closer to his own goal line than he thinks the kicker can kick the ball. If the kicker normally sends the kickoff to the 15-yard line, the return man would position himself on his own 5-yard line. One rule to never break is that the return man should not line up in his own end zone. He should never line up deeper than his own 1-yard line, just to be safe.

The return man's focus is on the kicking tee and the ball. He wants to see immediately where the kickoff is going. Once he sees the direction of the end-over-end flight of the ball, he changes his position to get directly in the path of the ball (figure 10.15a). He adjusts his forward movement to make the catch as he is going forward. To prepare for the catch, the return man places his little fingers together and brings the outside of his hands together with his palms, forming a catching basket for the ball (figure 10.15b). Both elbows are in close to his body. At the moment of the catch, the return man reaches out with his arms and hands in order to see his hands and the ball at the same time (figure 10.15c).

The instant he makes the catch, the return man secures the ball. If he is moving forward when he makes the catch, he will have momentum for the return. The return man must know where to run. Good kickoff return men not only know where they are supposed to run, they also understand the blocking that will be used on the return. Most long returns occur when the return man catches the ball and runs straight to a designated area of the field (figure 10.15d).

When making the catch and heading upfield, the return man looks for any small space to sprint through. This seam usually only appears for an instant, so he has to get through it as fast as he can. He should not hesitate, stop, or change direction when returning a kickoff. This can only get him in trouble, and it makes it hard for his teammates to get good blocks.

Kickoff return men need to remember that the kickoff is a free ball. Players from either team can fall on the ball and gain possession, including kicks that go into the end zone. The return man's focus should be only on making the catch. He must get to the ball and secure it before an opposing player can reach it. He should be prepared to fall on the ball, although he usually has time to pick it up and return it up the field. The return man should try to return every kickoff with abandon. He should head for the seam and have faith that his teammates will keep it open. He should never let the kicker make the tackle.

The return man must be alert for the short kick. On a short kickoff, the ball will hit the ground before the return man can catch it. As he moves forward to retrieve the short kick, the return man moves in front of the ball regardless of where it bounces. He concentrates on the ball, not on the opposing players.

Figure 10.15 Returning a kickoff: *(a)* return man gets in position; *(b)* he prepares his hands for the catch; *(c)* he makes the catch; *(d)* he starts up the field.

Punts

The punter's ability determines where a punt return man lines up. If the punter can kick the ball 35 yards, the return man should line up 40 yards behind the line of scrimmage. He wants to give himself room to move up and get under the ball to make the catch. This alignment also gives him protection in case the punter makes a really good kick. The farthest he should line up or catch a punt is his own 10-yard line. This is one rule to never break. Most punts that come down inside the 10-yard line will bounce into the end zone, creating a touchback, and will be brought out to the 20-yard line for the next play.

Because of the mass of players that are usually in front of the punter, the return man may not see the ball when it is kicked. The key is to locate the ball as soon as possible. Once he sees the ball, he should adjust his position to be in a direct line with the flight of the ball (figure 10.16a).

Once in position to make the catch, the punt return man comes under control with both palms up and the tips of his little fingers together (figure 10.16b). He cocks his wrist to form the catching area, and he reaches up with his arms and hands. He should see both hands and the ball at the moment of the catch (figure 10.16c). After catching the ball, the return man secures it and starts up the field (figure 10.16d).

When watching the ball in flight, the punt return man should try to see whether the front or the back of the ball is coming down first. On longer punts, the front point of the ball comes down first. This type of punt usually moves to the return man's right. If the back point comes down first, the punt is shorter. The return man has to come up farther, and the ball will sail to his left.

Not every punt has to be caught. Once the ball leaves the punter's foot, it is the opposing team's ball even if the return man does not catch it or if the kicking team downs it. The return man needs to think through the situation. If he does not feel that he can get in position to easily catch the punt, he should let it hit the ground and move away from it, yelling to his teammates to also move away from the ball. The other team can recover the ball if a player from the punting team falls on a bouncing punt after it has touched one of the return team's players.

While the punt is still in the air, the punt return man should prepare to signal a fair catch by waving one hand back and forth over his head (figure 10.17). A fair catch signal allows him to make the catch without being tackled. He cannot advance the ball after the catch, but his team does get the ball at the spot of the catch. He should consider making a fair catch signal when the punt is extremely high, the punt is a short kick that he can safely catch, or he senses that the cover men are right on top of him.

If he thinks he can gain yardage, the return man must be ready to run after the catch and to return the punt once the punt is caught and the ball secured. Before the ball is kicked, he must know where to return the punt if he gets a chance to run with the ball.

The kicker must be aware of the blocking that his teammates are going to use. Legal blocking on any kick return is hard. It is almost impossible if the return man does not return the punt to where his teammates think he will. He should try to return in the direction called by his coach. The one exception to this rule is if he has a right return call and the punt is kicked near the left sideline. In this case, if he can safely make the catch, it might be better to return up the left sideline. He may not have blocking and may not make many yards, but he will not be forced to run all the way across the field before turning and starting up toward the opponent's goal line.

Figure 10.16 Returning a punt: *(a)* return man gets in position; *(b)* he prepares his hands for the catch; *(c)* he makes the catch; *(d)* he starts up the field.

Figure 10.17 Signaling a fair catch.

Stopping, starting, and changing direction also cause the blockers trouble and hurt the return. Once he has secured the ball, the return man needs to turn on the speed, hit the return area as fast as he can, get as many yards as possible, and never let the punter make the tackle.

SPECIAL TEAM DRILLS

The drills for special teams usually include only a few players, but because of their importance, these positions must have practice time. For beginning punters and placekickers, begin by teaching the skills without the ball. Once the ball comes into the drill, it becomes the focus of the workout.

Placekicking

Purpose: To reinforce placekicking techniques.

Procedure:

1. The coach should review each segment of the placekicker's technique. The coach faces the kicker to observe his stance, steps, and kicking motion.

2. For the stance, the coach faces the kicker as the kicker lines up in his stance.

3. For the steps, the coach lines up in front and to the side of the placement spot to observe the kicker's motion. Don't use a tee or the ball; it is better to use a piece of tape as the placement spot.

4. To check the kicker's steps, the coach lines up in front and to the side of the placement spot.

5. The coach lines up 5 yards in front of the placement spot and observes the kicking motion, including the follow-through.

Coaching Points: The kicker needs to have his head and shoulders in front of his hips and his plant foot in the correct position. His kicking motion should be in a straight line. He should keep his eyes focused on the placement spot throughout his kick.

Short Snapping

Purpose: To reinforce proper technique when executing the short snap.

Procedure:

1. The coach lines up in front of the ball and observes the center's stance and grip.

2. After the center is comfortable with the proper stance and grip, the coach lines up as the holder or in front of the center to observe the center's snap.

Coaching Points: The center should have his hips even with his shoulders before the snap. The center must check that the holder is ready before the snap, have a good follow-through with both hands on the snap, and expect to block once the ball is released.

Holding for the Kick

Purpose: To reinforce proper technique for catching, placing, and holding the ball for the placekicker.

Procedure:

1. The coach lines up directly in front of the center.

2. The holder prepares to receive the snap.

3. When the center snaps the ball, the holder catches it and places it for the kick.

Coaching Points: The holder must be comfortable in his stance. The holder should catch the ball, move it to the placement spot, and adjust the laces and lean of the ball in one smooth motion. Some practice time should be spent fielding poorly snapped balls.

Punting

Purpose: To reinforce punting technique by focusing on each segment of the punt.

Procedure:

1. The coach lines up 15 yards in front of the punter and observes his stance, making corrections if necessary.
2. Once the stance is correct, the coach observes the punter's steps as he uses the two-step punting technique.
3. Once the stance and steps are correct, the coach observes how the punter sets up and places his hands to receive the snap. The punter should make sure he can see both the ball and his hands at the same time.
4. For the grip and drop, the coach stands to the side of the punter's kicking leg and hands him the ball. The coach observes the punter's grip and drop, making corrections if necessary.
5. The punter punts the ball, going through the entire motion.
6. To practice adjusting the nonkicking foot for directional punts, the coach sets up behind the punter, indicates the direction for the punt, and observes the punter's movement.
7. The center joins in the drill once the punter establishes the kicking motion.

Coaching Points: The punter must have a balanced stance, step on the balls of his feet, keep his shoulders in front of his hips, drop the ball onto his kicking foot correctly, and follow through with every kick. The techniques can be perfected individually and then combined without a ball. Next, the ball can be used without a center, and finally, the center joins in the drill. Punters should not kick with bad technique. Eliminate the ball if they are having trouble.

Long Snap

Purpose: To reinforce proper technique when executing the long snap.

Procedure:

1. The coach lines up directly in front of the center and observes his stance and grip.
2. After the center is comfortable with the stance and grip, the coach observes the center's snapping motion.

Coaching Points: Check that the front point of the ball is up before the snap. The center must see that the punter is ready and then fire the ball back to the punter. He needs good follow-through with both hands on the snap. After the snap he must be prepared to block and then cover down the field.

Kickoffs

Purpose: To reinforce proper kickoff technique by focusing on each segment of the kickoff.

Procedure:

1. The coach sets up to the side of the tee opposite the kicker's foot.
2. The kicker takes his stance and goes through his steps, making adjustments as necessary.
3. After mastering the stance and steps, the kicker goes through the approach and kicking motion without the ball as the coach observes.
4. Once the kicker is comfortable performing the motions without the ball, he can use the ball.

Coaching Points: Make certain that the kicker sets up in the proper location, that he attacks the ball keeping his head and shoulder in front of his hips, and that his plant foot is in the proper location to allow his leg to move through the kick. The kicking motion should propel the kicker's body forward. The kicker must concentrate on the tee and the ball all through the kick.

Returning Kickoffs

Purpose: To reinforce proper technique for returning kickoffs.

Procedure:

1. The coach lines up in the end zone behind the kick return man.
2. The return man uses the proper positioning, catch technique, and start.
3. Add the actual kick after the return man is set on the techniques for making the catch.

Coaching Points: The return man should position himself directly in front of the flight of the ball on every kick and be moving forward as he makes the catch. Make certain that he looks the ball into his hands on every catch. He must cover all kicks.

Returning Punts

Purpose: To reinforce proper technique for returning punts.

Procedure:

1. The coach lines up behind the punt return man.
2. The punt return man uses the proper positioning, catch technique, and start.
3. After the return man is set on the techniques for making the catch, he can use the ball.

Coaching Points: The return man should move quickly to get in front of every punt. He needs to determine whether to make the catch, call for the fair catch, or let the ball bounce. Make certain that he looks the ball into his hands on every catch. Throw the ball to the return man if the punter is not available or is inconsistent in his punts.

Index

Note: The italicized *f* following page numbers refers to a figure.

About the Author

Tom Bass coached for three NFL teams over a span of nearly 30 years. With the Cincinnati Bengals, Tampa Bay Buccaneers, and San Diego Chargers, he served as a defensive coordinator and assistant coach on both offense and defense, and he held the front-office roles of vice president of public relations and director of player personnel. Before his move to the NFL, Bass enjoyed six successful years of college coaching at San Jose State University and San Diego State.

Bass also is recognized throughout the world as a premier clinician. He conducts on-site technical football coaching clinics for football coaches from major colleges and universities as well as for youth, high-school, junior-college, and international coaches of American football. His football savvy is showcased in many venues: in his "In-Depth" clinics on his Web site www.CoachBass.com, in his "Ask the Coach" column on NFLhs.com, at "Tom Bass Football Seminars for Women Only," and through successful "Coach Bass Sports Maps" for NFL and college football.

As an ambassador of the game, Bass has served as president of the Sacramento Goldminers of the Canadian Football League and was on the board of directors for the International Football Federation of American Football, which covers four continents and 23 countries. Major corporations such as IBM, Coca-Cola, and Anheuser-Busch have hired him for his speaking talents, and he has been the featured guest on numerous sports talk and interview shows on radio and television, including HBO, ABC Nightly News, and ESPN.

Tom and his wife, Michele, live in Carlsbad, California.

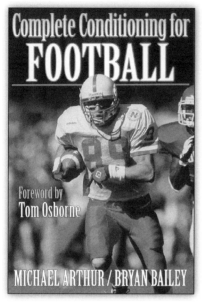
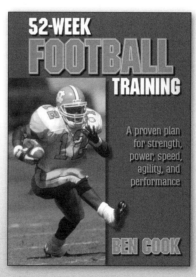